FAITH – A LIFE LONG COMPANION

notionpress
.com

FAITH – A LIFE LONG COMPANION

Ram Sehgal

notionpress.com

Notion Press

5 Muthu Kalathy Street, Triplicane,

Chennai - 600 005

First Published by Notion Press 2015

ISBN: 978-93-84391-48-5

In Gratitude to the Mother

"When the grace and protection of the Divine Mother is with you, what is there that can touch you or whom need you fear?

A little of it even will carry you through all difficulties, obstacles and dangers. Its touch can turn difficulties into opportunities, failure into success and weaknesses into unfaltering strength".

Sri Aurobindo

Acknowledgements

I am grateful to Sri Aurobindo Ashram Trust for permitting me to use the picture of The Mother.

Shri Manoj Das Gupta, the managing trustee of Sri Aurobindo Ashram, was instrumental in planting the idea which inspired me to write this book.

My wife Manju, helped me all the way while I was writing this book which took over two years .She went through chapter by chapter and made several suggestions and also corrected some facts. She enjoys a terrific memory!

My two good friends, Gautam Chatterjee and Sumer Sureka took the trouble to read the manuscript and assured me that the book was readable.

Finally, and not the least, the team at Notion Press who supported and guided me through the various stages: Co- founder- Naveen Valsakumar, Yamini Sekar- the Publishing Consultant, the Project Manager- Gracy Preeti Gomes- the Editor- Sandhya Sridhar, the Designer- Francis Bomban and the Typesetter- M. Gnanasoundari.

Foreword

I was a young Frenchman of barely 19 and I had no clue about India and its ancient wisdom. But then one day, a friend of mine told me that there was a caravan of cars driving from Paris to Pondicherry. And I thought: 'Why not? From Pondicherry, I can continue towards South East Asia, Japan, the USA, and come back to France after a year.'

But then, I stopped at Pondicherry because there I met the Mother, a French lady, who was Sri Aurobindo's spiritual companion and had taken over his work when he passed away in 1950.

The first time I met Her as an innocent 19-year-old, she looked deep into my eyes and in a split second, my whole world changed. I decided to live in India and devote the rest of my life to Her work.

When I met the Mother, she was nearly 90-years-old and had only four more years to live. Therefore, I was never able to spend much time with Her or talk with Her. I perhaps had just about seven private darshans.

Ram Sehgal by comparison, was a very privileged man. He came to the ashram as a child and had intimate, day-to-day contact with the Divine Mother when She was in Her body. Thus his testimony is unique, because many of those who met the Mother as children, have passed away and not many witnesses are left.

Not only that, Ram Sehgal is an accomplished man, who had a brilliant career, starting with Air India, becoming an icon of the advertising world and being nominated in 1998 as the Chairman of the Indian Advertising Standard Council.

This book is thus a very important document that will allow coming generations to get a unique glimpse into the Mother's life, She of whom Sri Aurobindo said: "Without Her I am Unmanifest".

Francois Gautier

Preface

When you are four-years-old, your life revolves around your parents. They enjoy your company as much as you do theirs. Sometimes, you create minor issues by demanding things which your parents believe are not good for you. Usually, both sides come to a compromise and the matter gets settled in a few minutes.

A year later, an intruder comes into your life in the form of a teacher. You are now trapped into a routine and you begin to dislike it. One more person who wishes to dominate you enters your life. The teacher even begins to influence your parents. You notice a change in your parents' behaviour towards you. They begin to nag you when you are still in your bed, fast asleep. When you return from school they begin to throw a volley of questions at you. It begins with, "What did you learn today?" and then goes on to, "Who are your friends?" Then they offer some snacks – it's almost always the same thing every day. This is practically shoved down your throat. For an hour or so, they leave you alone to play with the other children in the neighbourhood -

children who need to pass the scrutiny of your parents. Just when you are enjoying yourself for the first time in the day, you are called away. You are reminded of your teacher and the homework you had to do.

Between the ages of 12 and 16, the situation worsens. You are longing to become an adult as soon as possible. When you move into the 18-plus age group, a new word enters your life, a word that is so common these days: 'STRESS'. It starts to create trouble for parents who use another word to express their predicament known as 'tension'. Your life turns busy: a weekly test, followed by a monthly one and finally the fearful annual exam. If board exams were held every month, students would be the most religious community in the world!

After years of studying, you will look for a job. Now you enter a battlefield where only the fittest survive. This is the moment when you have to decide what you want to do in life. Your ambitions, your knowledge, your character, your attitude, your hard work and patience will all be on trial.

The vicious circle of life continues endlessly. You settle into a profession of your choosing if possible or, you accept whatever you can get.

Thanks to life's constant uncertainties, its twists and turns, all at varying speeds and frequencies, you seek dependable support.

Where does faith fit in?

There is a misconception that faith begins with experience. In reality, faith is not dependent on experience at all. To believe that faith comes with experience contradicts human psychology.

Sri Aurobindo writes, "All men of action, discoverers, and creators of knowledge proceed by faith and, until the proof is made or the thing done, they go on in spite of disappointment, failure, and disproof, because something in them tells them that this is the truth, the thing that must be followed and done."

Thousands of people belonging to various religions have faith before they experience it, and it is the faith that gives them the experience. As Sri Aurobindo says, "Faith is not intellectual belief but a function of the soul."

The first step in seeking support takes the form of a prayer. The next step is to seek peace of mind. While many things may be necessary to achieve peace of mind, one of the most important things is faith. For, faith ultimately leads to the development of an attitude of dependency on the Divine.

In this book, I am going to backtrack the journey of my life, going back 70 years. It starts when my parents settled at Sri Aurobindo Ashram in Pondicherry (called Puducherry now) in 1945. I grew up and lived there for 20 years. I then worked for over 40 years in different parts of the world and returned to Pondicherry in 2005.

It was a journey that took me through experiences that were not, by any means, a readymade bed of roses. All the adversity I've faced in life - troubles and obstacles - seemed to strengthen me. We may not realize it when it occurs, but it transforms us. Patience and perseverance have a magical effect, before which obstacles vanish. There is a certain flow of determination that rescues us and keeps us on track. Happiness is not the absence of problems; but rather, it is the ability to deal with them.

Hence, success is not measured by the position we have reached in life but by the obstacles that we were able to overcome by prayer and faith.

Contents

Chapter One

THE GLOWING YEARS

At the Sri Aurobindo Ashram

Sri Aurobindo was born in Calcutta on August 15, 1872. At the age of seven, he was sent to England along with his elder brother. There, he studied at St. Paul's School and later at King's College, Cambridge.

He returned to India in 1893, and worked for 13 years in the service of the Maharaja and as a professor at Baroda College.

In 1906, soon after the partition of Bengal by the British, Sri Aurobindo quit his post and moved to Calcutta (Kolkata). He soon became one of the leaders of the nationalist movement, and was the first to demand complete independence for India. Sri Aurobindo had begun the practice of yoga in 1905 at Baroda.

In 1910, he moved to Pondicherry, which was a French colony then. He withdrew from politics in order to devote his time entirely to his inner spiritual life and work.

During his 40 years at Pondicherry, he evolved a new method of spiritual practice, which he called the Integral Yoga. Its aim is a spiritual realization that not only liberates man's consciousness but also transforms his nature. In 1926, with the help of his spiritual collaborator, The Mother, he founded the Sri Aurobindo Ashram.

Among his many writings which run into 70 volumes, there are some prominent ones that include: 'The Life Divine', 'The Synthesis of Yoga', 'The Ideal of Human Unity', 'Essays on the Gita', and hundreds of letters that he wrote in reply to devotees around the world who sought his spiritual guidance.

Sri Aurobindo left his body on December 5, 1950.

The Mother was born Mirra Alfassa in Paris on February 21, 1878. Interested in occultism, she visited Tlemcen in Algeria in 1905 to study with Max Theon and his wife, who were practicing occultism. Her primary interest, however, was spiritual development. In Paris, she founded a group of spiritual seekers and gave talks to various groups.

In 1914, The Mother travelled to Pondicherry to meet Sri Aurobindo. She recognized him as the one who, for many years, had inwardly guided her spiritual development. After eleven months, she was obliged to return to France at the outbreak of the First World War. A year later, she went to Japan and stayed there for four years.

In April 1920, The Mother rejoined Sri Aurobindo. When the Sri Aurobindo Ashram was formed in November 1926, Sri Aurobindo entrusted its full material and spiritual responsibilities to The Mother. Under her guidance, which continued for almost 50 years, the Ashram grew into a large, many-faceted spiritual community. In 1952, she established the Sri Aurobindo International Centre of Education.

The idea of Auroville, the City of Dawn, was conceived by The Mother. She wrote the charter of Auroville for the international community who was seeking the spiritual guidance of The Mother. She wrote, "Auroville belongs to nobody in particular. It belongs to the humanity as a whole. But to live in Auroville one must be a willing servitor of the consciousness."

The Mother left her body on November 17, 1973.

My parents settled down at the Sri Aurobindo Ashram in Pondicherry when I was six-years-old and my brother was two. When my brother was five-years-old, there was a demand from my grandmother to have my brother's hair-cutting ceremony performed at Hyderabad. My father sought The Mother's permission. The Mother said, "Can anybody be more sacred than me? I will cut his hair!" We did not make the trip to Hyderabad and my father became an outcast in his family.

We grew up here and lived with our parents for twenty years. It is a unique spiritual institution which allows each one to follow their own path of self-development based on Sri Aurobindo's and The Mother's teachings.

I had been blessed with the greatest privilege of having a darshan of Sri Aurobindo.

It was on December 5, 1950, that Sri Aurobindo withdrew from his body. His body was glowing with a golden hue and the glow remained for five days. Thousands of people came from all parts of the world to have a final Darshan of him.

I can never ever forget his unique godlike face which is cast in my heart, mind and soul forever!

The Ashram is not a quiet place of retreat but a vibrant centre of life in a modern urban setting. The dynamic character of the community reflects the life-affirming aim of Sri Aurobindo's yoga. There are no obligatory practices, no rituals, no compulsory meditations or systematic instructions in yoga. He said, "All life is yoga."

At that time, there were fewer inhabitants in the ashram than they are today. They were provided accommodation, food, clothes, medicines and items of daily use. The people in the ashram were hard-working, dedicated and totally committed to whatever work The Mother had assigned them. They would do the same work for years.

Age was a never a bar to keep them away from work. This tradition continues even today. This dedication to work has become a hallmark of the institution and encompasses people from around the world, as well as from all parts of India.

The Mother was personally involved with all the activities of the various departments. Every day, she would meet with her secretaries and get briefed on issues and give them guidance.

The Mother took classes three days a week. They were divided into three groups: to children below the age of 14, she would relate stories written by her. She would also give dictations and correct the papers. The second level was boys and girls above the age of 18. Here, she would read selected portions of passages across a wide range of subjects and answer questions.

At the senior level of inmates, she would translate Sri Aurobindo's works from English into French. She played tennis every evening for an hour.

During the athletics season, she would visit the sports ground every evening and hold the string at the finishing line of the races. She would record the results of all the sporting events.

The Mother knew everybody by their first names and remembered their birthdays. On their birthdays, The Mother would give them a bouquet of flowers. Each person in the ashram would send her, in advance, a short list of books written by Sri Aurobindo and The Mother that they wished to read. These books were her birthday gift to them.

You could approach her whenever you had a problem. You could even write to her. You would receive a prompt reply and her blessings would resolve your problem. I cannot remember a single occasion when there was a need for me to pray.

For most people, God shapes the world by prayer. Faith and prayer are the driving force of the soul and people cannot live without them. We did not need either; we had The Mother physically in our midst.

We all felt like the chosen ones to be in her presence. She did not permit even our parents to interfere in our lives. She told them that she would be responsible for us. And this principle applied to all the parents who had been accepted as her disciples. My parents, for instance, would not know when I was running a temperature. I would inform The Mother or see her personally. I felt safe and relieved once I told her about it and would then return to my routine.

We lived a disciplined life. We were protected from outside influences and had nothing to worry about. In my Ashram life of 20 years, nothing seemed difficult. We lived in a peaceful environment. There was no caste, creed or religion. In fact, we did not know who came from which part of the country or the world. We knew each other by our first names. For instance, I did not know my surname until I needed it to get a passport to join Air India.

We were liberated and released from any pressures of religion, its rituals or practices. We were blind to the colour of skin as well. We had people from across the world with different complexions which went unnoticed.

The education system was totally different from that of any other place. No examinations were held at school or at the college. No degrees were handed over. The central government educational institutions accepted the certificates which carried no mark sheets. It created a love for learning with an absence of the tensions that usually accompany examinations. Those who wished to take up higher studies did not face much difficulty in competitive entrance examinations. In fact, the former students from this institution are spread across the world, involved in every profession: politics, law, finance, medicine, management, teaching, defence services, banks, media and advertising.

I chose to appear for the Baccalaureate examination in order to obtain a graduation degree. The preparation was hard and I had to read long hours during the day which gradually spread through half the night. As a result, I lost sleep for over a week. This was my very first experience of an examination. A senior inmate of the Ashram suggested that I should report the matter to The Mother. I went to see her and told her about the lack of sleep for over a week. The doctor had given me some sleeping pills and even that did not help. This is what she told me, "The body is capable of curing itself. It is only when you fill the body with medicine; the body loses its confidence!" She gave me a flower to bless me and placed her hand on my head. That night as soon as my head hit the pillow, I was dead to the world.

After the written examination, all the papers were sent to Paris for evaluation. Two weeks later, the results were declared and posted on the notice board of the French college. I had passed and had to appear for oral examinations, in three subjects, a week later. I fared well in the first two and during the third round, I felt giddy and fainted. My father took me back home.

The evaluations were being sent to Paris that very evening. So there was no way I could be examined again. Two weeks later, I found, to my utter surprise, that I had passed the examination. I went to see The Mother to inform her about the result.

She told me how it happened. The Ashram school director, a highly qualified French gentleman, was one of the jurors at the French college. He told The Mother what happened at that meeting. One of the professors decided to increase my marks by two The Mother looked at me and said, "It was the Divine's Grace." My immediate response to that was, "It was You, Mother". She smiled and blessed me.

I worked for five years in the afternoons at the Ashram workshop after my graduation. I spent the morning studying in the library. I took a writing course by correspondence from Regent Institute in London, and then began to write articles which were published in papers and magazines.

Now I was preparing to build a career. I was going to step into the outside world, of which I had no idea. I had no clue as to what kind of people I would be meeting in my life henceforth. My life, so far, had been protected like a Roman fortress.

Now, for the first time in my life, I found myself at crossroads. I had to safeguard and protect my faith as well as retain all that I had learnt from The Mother. At the same time, I needed to learn to pray.

Prayer is a very tricky thing. Man's view of God seems to be one-sided. We pray and want things to happen the way we see it. I knew that faith had a critical role to play in my life henceforth. I also needed to learn how to deal with prayers that remain unanswered. What I was certain of was that The Mother would give me what I needed but not necessarily what I wanted. I certainly needed The Mother's continuous grace and guidance to survive in an unfamiliar terrain. The change from a well-protected, peaceful and caring atmosphere into a self-centred and chaotic world was going to be tough.

Chapter Two

A Shaky Start

I asked my influential uncles who were senior government officers for help in getting a job. My parents had left their comfortable lives in a large town and moved to the Ashram. The family had not approved of their shift. Hence, I did not get any help from my uncles. I had to find my own way with The Mother's grace.

I realized that I had to look for a job by myself. The only advice I got from someone was, that I had to read the newspapers and check out the job vacancies listed there. Since I had a great desire to travel, I zoomed in on an advertisement from a shipping company. I dreamed of travelling by ship and seeing the world. I had no idea as to what to write to the company or what to say about myself. I decided to follow what I had been taught: to be honest. I wrote that I had no work experience but I promised to work hard. I knew that was not going to be enough. However, I did not feel any anxiety. I was even prepared not to receive any response. I was very much in The Mother's presence.

A week later, I got a letter from the shipping company, located in Madras (Chennai), to appear for an interview. I did not inform The Mother about this development. I was not quite sure whether I would get the job but I had a faint hope since it was a French company and I knew French.

I arrived at the office of the Maritimes Shipping Company an hour before the appointed time. I walked up to the reception desk and informed the lady that I had come for an interview. I was taken aback by her rudeness. "Did you read the letter which said 11:00 AM? Go there, join the queue and wait to be called." There were around twenty people waiting to be interviewed. A few minutes later, more people joined the queue. Peeping into my neighbour's papers, I gathered that he had listed his work experience. I had none. I told myself to be confident and that he would not know French. While I was involved in this debate with myself about the ultimate outcome of this trip, my name was announced.

As soon as I entered the room, a gentleman gave me a writing pad and a ballpoint pen. He began to dictate some text to me at high speed.

He noticed I was unable to cope with it. He stopped and asked me whether I had any experience with stenography. I was speechless.

He was kinder than the lady at the reception. He said, "I don't think you would enjoy doing a secretary's job!"

I returned to Pondicherry the same day. I did not share this experience with anyone. I had missed out on reading the word 'Stenographer' in the advertisement. What I read was: 'Maritimes Shipping Company' and I had begun to dream of travel. What a false start! I took a break from reading papers for a few days.

A month later, there was a large advertisement in a paper, from Air India.

They were looking for 'Flight Pursers' to work on the plane. I did not know what a purser did. However, I decided to send in my application.

Three weeks later, I received a letter from Air India asking me to appear for a written test in Madras. This time, my father decided to drive me there. We went a day earlier and stayed with my father's friend, Mr. Chettiar. The next day I reached the examination hall located in a hotel. Air India's notice was displayed in the reception. It listed all the names of those who were shortlisted for the test. To my horror, the list had 150 names. The candidates' list was broken up into three groups and the duration of the test was 20 minutes. I began to talk with some of the applicants. Nobody had a clue as to what kind of test it was going to be. One of the boys told us that the list covered the four southern states. Another boy told us what he had overhead in the toilet. One Air India official was telling another that 150 boys were appearing for four seats in the South.

The first ten minutes were devoted to mathematics. There were 25 questions in all and one had to tick the correct answer out of four options.

All I did was to tick answers randomly. It seemed like a visual test. There was absolutely no time to think! The English paper required us to write as many common words as we could beginning with the letter 'C'. I wrote 55 words within 10 minutes. Once the exam was over, everyone rapidly left the hotel. None of us was in the mood to discuss the exam.

My father enquired rather anxiously about how it all went. I said, "Let us pack our bags and go home!" These tests were even worse than lotteries! My father, however, was hopeful. All fathers keep their confidence alive in their offspring even when faced with dead-ends!

The results were to be announced the next day at the hotel lobby.

We packed our bags to return home the next day. My father insisted on dropping by at the hotel to check the selected list. I sat in the car and waited for him to return. A few minutes later, I saw my father running towards the car. I thought, since he had missed out on his morning jog, he was making it up with a run.

He almost screamed. "You are in!" I thought I had better check it out for myself and went in to examine the list. Yes! I was in! What my father did not read, though, was that the list of 50 selected boys had to go through interviews the next day. He thought I had got the job.

Since I had declared in my application that I knew French, the first interview was to establish beyond any doubt that I knew the language.

An Indian gentleman wished me good morning in French. I responded in French.

Then he asked me, "What is black market in French?" I was in top form. I replied immediately. "Marche Noir" - 'marche' means 'market' and 'noir' means 'black'. That was the end of the French test.

The next interview was directed towards general knowledge and was conducted by three people. It was tough to answer three people at the same time. Fortunately, I was well-trained by my parents who had the habit of asking me different questions at the same time. I would first reply to my mother and then to my father. Here, I chose to answer the chairman of the panel first. At the beginning of the interview, he had been kind enough to tell us his rank.

I went through one more interview that same day.

This was on general knowledge. The first question was, "What is a jumbo?' My answer was, "An elephant." I cannot remember the rest of the questions. However, apparently the answer to the first question was an airplane. Air India was in the process of acquiring large planes called 'Jumbo jets'.

The results would be known the next morning. One more day to enjoy our host, Mr Chettiar's delicious dosas!

Finally, four people were selected and I was one of them. We had to appear for a medical examination the next day.

On hearing the news, Mr. Chettiar decided to take us out to an expensive restaurant. He was indeed a caring and generous man.

The next morning, I had the medical examination. I was a sprinter who ran 100 meters in 12 seconds and 200 meters in 23.8 seconds. This was one moment in time where my self-confidence was at its peak.

I was medically disqualified on the grounds that I had a weak heart.

My host refused to accept the verdict of Air India's medical officer.

Mr. Chettiar was a friend of Madras city's best known heart surgeon. He drove me to his clinic. Dr. Cherian carried out a detailed examination for over an hour. He then called the Air India medical officer and informed him about his examination result. "The boy is outstandingly fit. It is a crime to disqualify a young man on a false health report. I will be reporting this matter to Air India!"

Less than a week later, I received a letter of appointment. On this entire journey, I had not prayed even once to The Mother for help. I was still living in the physical presence of The Mother. It was natural for me to leave it to her to decide my future.

On my return, I wrote to The Mother about all that had transpired and informed her that I had been selected for the job. I told her that I would not take the job if she did not approve of it. Within a few hours, someone brought a note written by her to me. The note was written in French. This is what she wrote, "Very good! It is an excellent occasion to see the world and enlarge your consciousness. Accept it, with my blessings."

Grace has a strange way of manifesting itself; it may even look like a sheer coincidence! How could anyone guess that Mr. Chettiar would know the best heart surgeon in town? Even a non-believer uncle of my mine, who came to know about my job, wrote to me, "This is indeed The Mother's Grace. How could you be selected, without any work experience, from among 150 other boys?"

It is from here onwards that my actual journey of faith began. I knew that faith alone would not make my journey easy. But it would give me the strength and confidence to face all the obstacles. I would be able to treat each obstacle as an experience. I had no doubt that The Mother let me go so that I could be enriched by my experiences.

Chapter Three

The Flying Years

I joined Air-India on August 17, 1963. This was my first visit to Bombay (Mumbai). I was rather nervous because I was scared of the big city. I had requested my cousin who was working in Bombay, to pick me up at the station. This was also my first travel by train. For that matter, it was for the first time that I was wearing trousers and a full-sleeved shirt. A tailor known to my father stitched three trousers in four days for me.

I stayed with my cousin for two weeks while I looked for accommodation. My cousin's flat was small and I did not wish to inconvenience him and his family. One day, during the lunch break, I saw an Air India official sticking a paper on the notice board. I went up to read it thinking it would be a set of instructions for us. It was an advertisement for a paying guest accommodation. I found out who the owner was. He was an employee of Air India. I walked up to him and told him I was looking for a place. He asked me to meet him at an address that evening. As I waited at a bus stop a gentleman stopped his car and asked me to hop in. He turned out to be the owner of the house. He showed me a room with sea view and an attached bath. I was quite excited since it was not too far from the training centre and I could cycle to the office. I moved in the very next day. Right opposite the house was a little Iranian restaurant. My food requirements were taken care of. A week later, I noticed that there was a laundry just below my window. I could get my uniform laundered without having to leave my room.

Now all my needs were met. It was like being back at home!

I began the training sessions at the cabin crew office. There were 22 participants, half of them were air hostesses and the rest were pursers. There were only two people who knew a foreign language: Haridas Mukherjee and myself. We were separated from the rest of the group and sent to a fast-track training program which would be conducted for one month while the rest of the batch would spend two months.

I was shocked beyond words when I was told about what we would be taught. We were taken to the airport hangar to learn about the plane's emergency landings on sea and land. We participated in a drill that lasted an entire week. We were taught how to handle the emergency equipments. We were dropped up and down by a shute. We learnt to demonstrate the life belts and oxygen masks to passengers prior to take-off.

The next part of the training was in the galley of the plane. We were taught by the catering manager all about food and wine. We even learnt how to heat food and place it on the plate for the hostess to serve to the passengers. We had to remember what wines should be served with the appetizers and what with the soup. However, this gets complicated with the main meal. The choice of wine differs with fish, chicken and red meat. For someone who had never tasted any alcohol and was vegetarian, this whole exercise seemed pointless!

We were then sent to the administrative department to learn about documentation that we needed to carry out on flights: immigration rules, customs procedures and preparing reports of every flight and notes on passenger complaints.

Finally, we were told how to deal with the passengers. The list had far more don'ts than dos'. They seemed simple enough not to warrant a training session. Just check out the list: keep full control of yourself; never ever lose your temper with a passenger no matter how he provokes you; never drink on the flight; do not sleep on the plane during the long haul night flights. I have not listed all of them but this would give you an idea.

At the end of the training program, I was put on a flight from Bombay to Hong Kong as a trainee purser. I was back in two days. Three days later, I was sent on another sector - Bombay to Cairo. I mailed a postcard from Cairo to The Mother describing my experiences of the two cities. And whenever I visited the Ashram, I would get to see her in her room. I would offer her French perfume on every trip. The first one I gave her was called Je reviens (I will return) and the next perfume was called Prophecy. She smiled when she read these names. She opened the bottle and sprayed a bit on the back of her palm and smelt it. This was the first time I discovered how perfumes should be checked for their fragrance!

The fast track movement of Grace continued... I was confirmed and put on regular flights to work on my own. I continued to send picture postcards to The Mother from every city I visited. I had mailed her postcards about my travels from my first flight until I quit Air India four years later. It covered over 25 cities around the world.

On my first birthday outside the Ashram, The Mother sent me a note, "Happy birthday, with my blessings that Sri Aurobindo's protection be always with you." She had even written my cousin's address on the envelope. My cousin never parted with that cover; it had his name written by The Mother!

After I completed one year of service, I was entitled to two weeks leave. I visited the Ashram and sought The Mother's permission to marry an Ashram girl, Manju. She too had come to the Ashram when she was very young. She was a very good student and an outstanding sportswoman. Both of us went to see The Mother. The Mother placed a mangalsutra around Manju's neck and also gave her a red Benarasi saree that had been worn by her. She blessed us both by placing her hand on our heads. Then she said, "This is your home, come back!"

I was entitled to two free air tickets after completion on one year. I got a free ticket to take Manju with me to Bombay. This was Manju's first experience of air travel. I have flown with many first time-flyers. They are nervous wrecks and expect us to hold their hands during take-off and landing. Manju shrugged off my hand when the plane was taking off. After all, she was a champion diver and jumped off a 15-meter high diving board. Perhaps, she felt that the plane was flying 15 meters high!

My cousin received us at the airport with flowers. He vacated his bedroom for the newlywed couple. I had to vacate my paying guest accomodation since it was a bachelor's den.

When I rejoined work I was called by the chief flight purser. He said the company had decided to send us on honeymoon to Hong Kong.

This posting was unprecedented since the company sent people out of the country only after 18 months of work experience.

My wife did not have a passport and I could not leave her alone in Bombay. This was the first time she had left Pondicherry.

I went to the passport office and applied for her passport. I submitted the form and was told that it would take over a month. I panicked. Manju and I sat down on a bench in the passport office wondering what to do.

While I was looking at the names of the officers on their doors, I noticed a surname which was the same as mine.

As I moved towards that door, Manju reminded me to pray to The Mother. I did so for a few minutes and then knocked on the door. I walked in. The gentleman looked rather surprised and irritated by my behaviour. You do not walk in unless you are called. And there were at least a hundred people waiting in the queue. With a great deal of nervousness I announced my name and sought his help. I explained my situation to him. He softened up, called for the concerned clerk and instructed him to issue the passport within a week. We were stunned for a few minutes and we had tears in our eyes. The Mother had intervened and got us out of an impossible situation.

We left for Hong Kong the following week, and now we were on course, adjusting ourselves to our new life.

In Hong Kong we found a small apartment with an attached toilet but we had to share the kitchen with three other Chinese families. The time for each family's cooking during the day was amicably settled by the landlady. She first asked the Chinese families to name their time of convenience. What was left of the day was good enough for my wife to cook dinner. We had breakfast and lunch in a restaurant conveniently located within the building complex.

I had to fly twice a week from Hong Kong to Tokyo. I asked Manju whether she would like to visit Tokyo on my next flight. She jumped up and said, "Yes, of course, I would love to!" She stayed two nights in the hotel with me. Thereafter, I fixed a room in YWCA, which was located right in front of the hotel. The day I left Tokyo, I checked her in and told her I would be back in four days to pick her up.

Four days later, I entered the reception of the ladies' hostel, picked up the guests' telephone and rang her room. There was no response. I went up to the receptionist and enquired about the occupant of the room. She looked up, surprised at my question, and simply said, "She has gone," and handed over a letter. I was in a deep shock and hence unable to open the envelope. The receptionist was a graceful old lady and she helped me open the envelope. Manju's note said that she had joined a tour of Japan and would be back in nine days! I whispered to myself, "Look at this crazy girl who has stepped out for the first time from Pondicherry and is off to tour Japan on her own!"

She came back with a fashionable Japanese shirt for me to appease my anger. She had bought her first camera. She showed me the pictures that she had taken of places of interest. She had also taken pictures of her tour group members. Overnight, she had turned into a world traveller!

Two weeks later we returned to Bombay. Before we left Hong Kong, we bought a small refrigerator to save Manju from buying vegetables every day. Furthermore, we did not have to pay for any excess baggage since we were returning from a posting. Hong Kong, no doubt, was the cheapest place in the world to buy expensive white goods.

Just three days before we were to leave, a New Zealander in our building committed suicide. Nobody had any information about his family. He was our neighbour but had never interacted with us. He was a loner.

The police made some enquiries and failed to get any clues. One of the police officers approached me and offered to sell the man's Lambretta scooter to me. The price was very attractive. I bought it without having to worry about any excess baggage charges. My wife, being more pragmatic than I was, reminded me about the Indian customs duty. I said, "We will deal with it when we get there. For now just imagine that we will no longer need to wait at bus stops!"

Back in Bombay my flight duties took me to London with a night halt at either Cairo or Beirut. I also flew from Bombay to Hong Kong with two night halts. At the end of the fifth month, I was posted at London.

Unlike Hong Kong, a British colony then, London was an expensive city. Apartment rents were very high and we had to be careful about our living expenses. Once we had settled the issue of meeting our living expenses, we began to visit shops. It was fairly easy to avoid expensive purchases since we did not have the money to do so. At the end of posting our suitcases weighed exactly the same as when we had left from Bombay.

However, the stay in London had high educational value. We could see places that we had read about in our history books and in English novels. London is, perhaps, one of the most historic and cultural cities in the world. It is also a very exciting city. Six months was not enough for us to visit the many famous places in England. We had only weekends to ourselves. However, we managed to visit some of the interesting places. We went to the Tower of London where celebrities had been either imprisoned or beheaded, to the home of William Shakespeare at Strafford-on-Avon. Incidentally, a bust of Rabindranath Tagore was placed in Shakespeare's garden. The Westminster Abbey was where Princess Diana got married and where the funeral rites of some prominent British citizens have been held.

We visited the two most famous universities of England: Oxford and Cambridge. They were home to awe-inspiring buildings surrounded by beautiful gardens. We spent a longer time at Cambridge because Sri Aurobindo had studied there. It was a pilgrimage for us.

The cultural life was exciting too: theatres that put up famous plays, antique and gracious old cinema halls screened old films... A visit to Madame Tussaud's Wax Museum was quite thrilling. Here you could come face to face with some of the world's most famous people - from Winston Churchill to Mahatma Gandhi. And, of course, a visit to certain parts of the Buckingham Palace to enjoy the extravagant antique furniture and paintings of reputed artists. And a sightseeing tour of Harrods, the famous and the most expensive department store in Britain. It was here that Queen Elizabeth and Princess Diana shopped.

Finally, one could not resist watching a tennis match at Wimbledon and a cricket match at the Lord's cricket ground!

Over weekends we listened to speakers spread across Hyde Park. They stood on small soap boxes and spoke on the least important topics of the week and amused people. We did not stick to one speaker but heard them all, by turn. What was really impressive was that the size of audience did not affect their enthusiasm. They would not stop speaking even if there was just one person who was looking at him and perhaps not even listening. We visited the extraordinary artistic display of flowers at the palace gardens. The famous dog shows were very popular and well-attended, displaying the love the English had for dogs. The dog that won the heart of spectators was chosen on the basis of the loudest cheers it received. The victorious dog would be garlanded by the chief guest. Its owners would also be cheered on by the spectators.

The beauty of London was that both pomp and simplicity had their own individual spaces.

Chapter Four

The Air India Experience

At the end of three years with Air India, I began to feel restless - I was tired and bored. What I was doing became mechanical and monotonous. The regimentation of flight duties did not permit me to plan even one week of other activities. Every Friday we would get the flight duties for the following week. We would take a flight which kept me away from home for two nights. Thereafter, we would be placed on stand-by duty. If a cabin crew reported sick we would be called to take the flight at short notice. We had to keep our bags packed and uniform ready. Moreover, I was not learning anything new either.

There were two aspects to The Mother's permission: see the world and expand your consciousness. In five years I had travelled quite extensively: Singapore, Hong Kong, Tokyo, London, Paris, New York, Cairo, Beirut, Rome, Dubai and Teheran. It would have taken people many years to cover these cities.

It was the second part of The Mother's message that was beginning to trouble me.

You can't always pretend to take life into your own hands when you are facing struggles. You need to leave it to the Divine to intervene.

I prayed to The Mother to guide me. I decided to meditate every night before I went to sleep. It helped me to distance myself from my worries. One morning I woke up with a start. I figured out that I was completely missing out on a golden opportunity to learn more about human beings: their behaviour and attitudes. I had the opportunity to study people who belonged to different parts of the world with different backgrounds. I realized that I could gain by my understanding of human behaviour and perhaps could use this knowledge in the future. I could not possibly take credit for this thought. It was all The Mother's guidance.

I began in earnest to observe and interact with the passengers. This activity was beyond the call of my duty. My first insight was that people differ by their background and occupation. I began to categorize my experience on this basis.

The first class passengers belonged to different categories: politicians and bureaucrats; industrialists; celebrities, actors, musicians, well-known sportsmen and authors.

The economy class travellers were often difficult to categorize. They belonged to almost every income category: contract labourers flying to the Middle East; middle level executives on brief assignments; parents visiting their children settled abroad and some well-to-do families on holidays.

The Politicians

Mr. Krishna Menon, the then Defence Minister of India, was flying back from London after representing Mr. Nehru (who was ill at the time) at the Commonwealth Conference. We were cautioned in London by the Air India staff to handle him with great care. The flight was scheduled to fly from London to Bombay, via Beirut. When we were an hour away from Bombay, he waved his hand and called me. He talked loudly enough to be heard by all the passengers seated in first class who had perhaps failed to recognize him. "Tell the pilot to fly to Delhi; I have an urgent meeting with the Prime Minister of India!"

I went to the cockpit and said, "Captain, Mr. Krishna Menon wants you divert the flight to Delhi. He says he has to meet Mr. Nehru urgently!"

"Who is this guy?" he asked.

"Who? Nehru or Menon?" I enquired rather politely, not knowing the depth of the Captain's knowledge of politicians.

"Nehru I know!" he snapped back.

"Mr. Menon is the Defence Minister of India."

"Then why he is on this flight? He should have taken a direct flight to Delhi."

I thought it was a very logical question. I returned to Mr. Menon and said, "The pilot is not authorized to alter the flight plans. You will have to take a connecting flight from Bombay for Delhi, sir." He snapped back, "Did I ask for your advice? Tell the pilot I will get him sacked." I decided not to pass on Mr. Menon's threat to the captain. In anger, he might decide to crash land!

However, the captain had second thoughts and said, "Tell him I will fly as close to Delhi as possible and he can jump out with the help of a life jacket. After all, he is the Defence Minister of India - he should be able to do that!"

Two weeks later, I was hauled up by the Manager of passenger services and reprimanded for being rude to the Defence Minister. C'est la vie!

However, another experience within a month helped to calm my feelings for this tribe.

Mr. Lal Bahadur Shastri, the then Prime Minister of India was travelling to Cairo to attend the Non-Alignment conference. Before he went to sleep, he asked me wake him up thirty minutes prior to landing in Cairo. I remembered this request only when the pilot had switched on the seat-belt sign. We were to land in 15 minutes. I was a nervous wreck. I went to his seat and switched on the reading light. He was obviously a light sleeper and woke up immediately. I said, "I am extremely sorry I forget to wake you up, sir. We will be landing in 15 minutes." He smiled and said. "That's good. Now I will have to write and read out a short speech at the airport!"

One more unexpectedly good experience was with Mrs. Indira Gandhi. One had heard that she was a tough person to deal with. The entire crew waited at the door of the aircraft at 11:30 PM at Bombay airport. Mr. Tata, the chairman of Air India, was also standing at the door.

First, he supervised the arrangements made for her bed. He then moved to the galley to check out the food arrangements. I had never before seen such a spread of sandwiches and juices in my life. Around 3:00 AM, Mrs. Gandhi went to the toilet. I requested the hostess to ask her when she came out, if she would want something to eat or drink. The hostess asked her, "Madam would you like to have something to eat or drink?" She replied with a smile, "Oh! I just had some water inside the toilet, thank you!"

And, incidentally, let the reader know that we kept filtered water in the toilet!

The sandwiches and juices remained intact. None of us could touch them because a stern note was stuck to the trays. It read, "Only for Prime Minister's personal use!"

The Members of Parliament

A group of eight MPs were travelling from Delhi to Geneva. They were enjoying themselves, drinking and talking loudly in the aisle. Some passengers complained about the noise. I requested them to be seated and to talk softly. They were annoyed and threatened to complain to the Air India management about my rudeness. However, reluctantly, they moved into the galley area and converted the place into a bar.

The Royalty

The British Royalty's behaviour is deep-rooted in tradition and has evolved over many centuries. Hence it is unique and exemplary in character. Lord Louis Mountbatten and his daughter were travelling from

Delhi to London. Their demeanour was astonishing. They were exceedingly polite and thanked the hostess every time she served them food or a drink. The entire crew on the flight was full of praise for them.

I had developed the habit of requesting autographs of well-known personalities. I requested him for his autograph. He took the book from my hand and passed it on to his daughter for her autograph. Once she had finished, he signed and gave it back to me.

There seems to be something in common between the British Royalty and the Indian Maharajas. The Maharaja of Mysore was travelling to London. He was indeed a gracious and humble human being. He chatted with me for a few minutes and enquired about our flight duties. He appreciated the cabin service. I told him, "It is nicknamed the Maharaja Service." He laughed loudly!

The common man

The most well-behaved people on the plane were in the economy class. They were respectful and kept to themselves most of the time. They might have been a bit nervous about the way they were supposed to eat their meals: for some, the use of the fork and knife was puzzling. Family members with children enjoyed themselves. The hostesses kept the kids occupied with games and ice cream through the flight. We were all happy to watch them having fun. We rarely faced any problems with economy class passengers.

Another charming experience was on a Gurkha soldiers' chartered flight. These men belonged to the British army. Once in two years, they were flown from Hong Kong to Calcutta on holiday. Nepal Airlines would fly them to Kathmandu. When the food was being served by the air hostesses, they would get up a little from their seats to show respect to the girls. The girls, of course, were happy with these gestures.

Air India management

For the crew, among the most feared passengers on Air India were two gentlemen - the Chairman, Mr. J.R.D Tata, and the commercial director, Mr. S.K. Kooka. We were alerted in advance that these two gentlemen were going to be on the flight. They were tough, exacting perfectionists and would not tolerate a single mistake. Everything had to be just right. For instance, Mr. Tata once slept through an entire Bombay-Geneva flight, including a 45-minute refuelling halt at Beirut. On landing at Geneva airport, he asked me to call the Air India airport manager. The Swiss gentleman climbed the step ladder rather nervously. Mr. Tata said to him, "Send a telex message to the Beirut manager and ask him why the ashtrays were not cleaned in the economy class on ground."

Mr. Kooka was equally particular about the crew's handling of passengers. The cabin crew was scared of passenger complaints. Mr. Kooka took strict action if the complaint was justified. The crew could be suspended or the monthly efficiency bonus would be deducted.

The Air India experience

The Mother got me into Air India. It was her immense grace and intervention that made it possible against all odds. Thereafter, every single experience laid the foundation for my future career. To observe, learn and interpret people's attitudes needs a lot of patience and pays off in the long run.

My experience with Air India gave me, quite literally, a flying start in life. There were many facets to this learning experience. When one is young, one does not easily adapt to the concept of discipline. Somehow, one feels robbed of freedom. However, if discipline is enforced and helps to keep one's job, one is less likely to be resentful. The concept of discipline was already very much a part of my upbringing at the Ashram. As part of the flying crew, I had to be punctual and ready 30 minutes before pick-up time. The uniform had to be laundered after every flight and the shoes had to be polished as well. Not too many jobs demand that you organize your life according to a manual!

In most jobs one does not deal with a hundred people at a time. My job required me to do just that and sometimes for continuous stretches of eight hours at a go, and at least, twice a week.

It was a crash course in understanding human nature while being quick on your feet. Each person needed a different kind of treatment.

There was also an interesting learning. We had to be equally patient with the arrogance of the rich and the crudeness of the not-so-rich. You could not carry any kind of racial biases. This aspect of human character I had already learnt at Pondicherry.

This continuous process of learning kept me in Air India for another two years. I now wanted to widen my horizon and was in a position to seek another career. All that I had learnt at Air India made me a better person.

I learnt: punctuality, discipline, the ability to handle people with different characters and behaviour, to listen to people attentively and show your concern, breaking no rules, and finally, to be truthful in all the flight reports that were sent to the headquarters after every flight. It was almost like a degree in management for free!

I knew that The Mother would find a way for me to move forward. Her Grace had got me into Air India. The Air India experience was priceless and had prepared me for the next phase in my career development.

Chapter Five

The Hunt For A Career

While I continued to pray to The Mother about my future career, I met an American on a flight from London to New York. He was the media director of a leading advertising agency in New York. After dinner, he came across to the crew rest area and sat next to me. We began to chat. He looked at me and asked, "What are your plans for the future? You are too bright to be in this job for long." That set the ball rolling. I told him that I was keen to join the advertising profession. He advised me to take up an advertising course in London from the Institute of Practitioners in Advertising. I took the course and completed it in one year. He had given me his business card and asked me to contact him after I finished the course.

Pampered passengers are usually generous at a height of 30,000 feet without realizing the pitfalls of their actions. I called him in New York after a year, after one of my flights. At first, he could not place me, and I had to relate a joke that he shared with me. That did it! I went to meet him. He sent me to meet the HR head for a discussion. The lady spoke too fast with a strong American accent, and I failed to follow a single word in spite of my best efforts. This was an aborted start to a career in New York.

Having failed to enter the advertising arena in New York, I decided to make an attempt in London. I paid a visit to the J. Walter Thompson's office at 40 Berkeley Square. I was sent to meet one of their junior executives. He began, "So you are from India? Jolly good! How is the advertising business in India? Is it growing or declining? How many agencies are there?" I was clueless. I replied rather meekly, "I have just completed the IPA exams I know nothing about the advertising scene in India. I am looking for a break in advertising." He said, "Oh! I was told you were a journalist!" He seemed disappointed. He was kind enough to take me to the HR head's office and left me there for further discussions.

This time I met a gentleman who wore a three-piece grey suit and smoked a pipe while drinking black coffee. He appeared to be ready to go out for a business lunch. In a pompous voice, he said, "All right young man, what is it that you want from me?" I blurted out, "I want to be in advertising, sir."

"I'll tell you what. When you get back to Bombay, call this bloke Greg Bathon who runs the Thompson Company in India. Go and see him."

A couple of weeks later, I returned to Bombay. I called Mr. Bathon's office and told his secretary about my meeting with the gentleman in London. She said, "This week he is busy, please call back next week." I replied,

"I don't have a phone, when can I call?" She asked me to hold on and got back in a few minutes to confirm a meeting for Tuesday at 11:00 AM. (For those readers who are not as old as I am and wondering why I didn't have a phone - I was waitlisted and was informed that the waiting period to get a phone connection was about 10 years!)

On Tuesday, I reached the Thompson's office, as usual, ahead by 45 minutes. This time around I was in for a surprise. I was ushered into the room within five minutes. There was a young man standing by the window sipping from a cup. "I am sorry. I am in the wrong room!" I said. "I have come to meet Mr. Bathon."

"I am Bathon," he said with a smile. I was stunned to see a young man heading the Thompson agency in India. He heard me out with patience. Then he said, "We are in the process of reorganizing our structures. It will take a couple of weeks. There will surely be an opportunity of an opening for you. Stay in touch."

I could not wait any longer. My wife was pregnant, expecting our first child and I could not be flying around the world while she was left all alone to look after herself. I needed a ground job. I was desperate. Faith is an excellent guide and teacher. Faith is believing when it is beyond the power of reason to believe. Faith has strange ways of manifesting itself. There are times when we need to pray for strength to bear our problems.

This was the moment to pray for The Mother's intervention.

Three weeks later, I was on a flight from London to Bombay. On this flight a young lady became airsick.

I gave her some medicine from the first-aid kit, and put her on oxygen for a few minutes. I returned to the crew rest area. An hour later, the young lady came and sat beside me. She thanked me for taking care of her. We began to chat. Normal stuff you talk about with a stranger - "Which part of Bombay do you live in? What are you studying and in which college?" In the course of the conversation, I asked her, "What does your father do?"

She said, "He is in advertising and is chairman of Lintas." I gasped, "My God!"

"What happened? Is it such a bad thing to be in advertising?"

I hastened to say, "NO, NO! I want to be in advertising myself!" She was relieved and offered to set up a meeting with her father. She gave me her phone number and asked me to call her the next day.

I met the chairman in the afternoon. He too did not have any vacancy. However, being introduced by his daughter, he showed some consideration and offered to call Mr. Peter Palmer, chief executive of S. H. Benson, a British agency. He fixed an appointment right away. He told me how to get to Benson's office.

As soon as I reached the office of the agency, I was ushered into Mr. Palmer's office. He was smoking a pipe. He was pleased to learn that I had studied advertising in London. He even offered me a cup of coffee. In a clipped upper British accent, he said, "You are in luck, young fellah! Our Calcutta Manager is here and is looking for young people to join his team in Calcutta." He rang the bell for his secretary. "Take this young man to see our manager from Calcutta." I was relieved to learn that I was not being sent to see another HR head!

Later I learned that Mr. Palmer was a retired pilot from the British Royal air force. His plane had been shot down by the Germans in the Second World War and he had lost the use of his legs. I did not even realize that he was seated in a wheelchair. A remarkably handsome and gracious gentleman!

The Calcutta manager was courteous. He asked me whether I had any relatives living in Calcutta. I said, "My wife is Bengali. Her brothers live in Calcutta and her parents are in Bishnupur." He smiled and said, "That will help!" He offered me the job but warned me that I would not be paid as much as I was in Air India. I would be on probation for six months. If I performed well during this period, my salary would likely be increased. He asked, "When can you join?" I said I needed to give Air India a month's notice.

I returned home and told my wife that I had got the job. She took it for granted that the job was in Bombay. I had to break the news gently to her since she loved Bombay. I said, "We have to move to Calcutta. I know you will be upset. But when our child is born, we will have your entire family to help you!" Her reply astounded me, "You wanted to change your job and I am very happy you got it. When do we leave?" I told her that we still had a month to organize ourselves. From that moment on, Manju stood by me all my life. Later on in my career, we had to move around several cities of the world!

I went to the Air India office to submit my resignation. The Personnel Manager was taken aback. "What upset you?" he asked. I replied, "Nothing really, sir. I am joining an advertising agency." And then he said, "You are the first person ever to resign from the flying job!" He shook my hands rather warmly and wished me well. I completed my notice period of 30 days.

Our lawyer friend managed to rent out our flat. We packed our bags and left by train for Calcutta.

Chapter Six

The Highs and the Lows
The Calcutta Experience

We reached Calcutta on October 18, 1967. We were met by Manju's elder brother. He was a senior engineer at Calcutta Improvement Trust (CIT). While reading the newspaper the next day, I realized that we could not have chosen a worse time to live in this city. I had never heard of Naxalbari before. It was a string of villages in Darjeeling district, tucked away in the foothills of the Himalayas. It was some 600 kilometres from Calcutta. Most of the villagers were tribal peasants who worked in plantation estates. They were manipulated by rich landlords and pushed off from fields and denied the revenue due to them. Deprived of subsistence wages, some died for lack of food. These villagers were forced to become militant and fight for their rights. They armed themselves with country-made guns and ammunition. This movement reached Calcutta fairly quickly and the militant revolt gained the support of young students who gave up their studies and joined them.

We lived with my brother-in-law in Dumdum for three months. This area was the stronghold of the Naxal movement. One night we went to visit Manju's uncle who lived close by. We were shocked to see two young boys carrying guns enter the house. They placed the ammunitions under a bed and left. The uncle then explained what was going on in his house. They belonged to the Naxal group and most of the boys had left their homes to seek shelter elsewhere. Manju's aunt would give them dinner; they would sleep in their house and leave very early in the morning. This had been a daily routine for over 18 months apparently. In return, the family got the necessary security. A few weeks later we learnt that one of the boys was shot down by the police in front of Manju's uncle's home.

My brother-in-law found us a two-bedroom apartment. Its location was somewhat unsettling. The lane in which it was located was surrounded by hut dwellers. At sunset, the earthen ovens would be lit across the entire lane, creating a lot of smoke. We had to keep our windows closed till their cooking was over. We were also not welcomed by the neighbourhood. Our disadvantage was that we were owners of a car and I had to blow my horn to clear the lit earthen ovens from the middle of the road when I was returning home from office. However, within a few weeks, we began to benefit by our location. The men-folk of the locality made a living through certain skills: they were electricians, plumbers, masons and painters. All I had to do, while driving to the office, was to stop in the middle of the lane and shout the name of the person I needed help from. The other voices of the neighbourhood would carry the message to the concerned person.

Life is about experiences that teach one many useful things: for instance, respect the poor, it is not their fault that they live a life of poverty. My wife and I made some friends in our neighbourhood. In a small way we helped some of them to make money.

I joined the agency, and the first thing I did was to place a large picture of The Mother on the wall of my room. I have done this in every office that I occupied in any city in the world until my return to Pondicherry. Now all these photographs are in our house!

The office was situated in the heart of the town. It took me 45 minutes to cover a distance of 6 kilometres. To arrive and return safely was a herculean task. I had to avoid trams, trucks, cars, motorcycles cycle rickshaws, cows and abusive pedestrians. In Calcutta, everyone had special rights to use the roads in whatever way suited them.

One evening, when I returned from the office, we heard gunshots just under our balcony. Manju and I were completely shattered. A young man who was drinking some water from the roadside tap was shot dead by a policeman. His body was left on the road. We were scared. My office colleagues advised me not to speak with anyone I did not know. Apparently, there were informants on both sides: the police and the students had created a network across all the localities of Calcutta.

I found safety in the office. It was not a big office and had a staff of around forty people. I began work in full earnest and spent long hours at work. I had learnt the theories relating to marketing and advertising principles in my course in London. However, this turned out to be a handicap. My boss was not educated on the subject. I was told he taught English at Calcutta University. He had joined the organization a few weeks before I did. I was made his assistant. However, he had no idea how to deal with clients. He took me to every single meeting. He was given charge of some of the agency's large clients. However, he was unable to deal with the flow of work within the agency and was also unable to brief the creative people about the communication needs of the clients.

A few weeks later, to everyone's surprise, he stopped coming to office. None of us were told about his exit. The manager of the office called me and informed me that he would be handling the clients himself and I would be his assistant. This rattled me. I knew he would be busy managing office affairs and I would be held responsible for any potential mishap with a client. I went home and told Manju about it. She simplified my problem. She said, "Air India taught you how to handle hundreds of difficult people. The Mother's grace has created this opportunity for you. Thank her and just focus on the job and work hard! If the manager is happy with your work, you will progress faster."

Whenever I had spare time I would spend it with the various department heads. They would teach me the key details of their work. In about six months, I was able to follow work through the agency quite easily. My keenness to learn from them helped me to build a close rapport. They went out of their way to help meet my deadlines with the clients. This led the manager to give me independent charge of the business I was handling as an assistant.

On March 7, 1968, my elder daughter, Reshmi was born. My parents came from Pondicherry and Manju's parents came from Bishnupur to bless her. It was indeed a joyful gathering of both the families.

A year later, I received a notice from the housing society in Bombay where I had bought a small apartment. Apparently, the tenant was running a brothel in our flat. We were asked to get him out within two weeks.

The next day I sought a meeting with the manager of the office. I explained my position and requested him for a transfer to the Bombay office. He was sympathetic and promised to speak with the managing director, Jack Hawthorne. However, he said, "You will need to stay on for a month to hand over the business to another executive."

A week later, he confirmed that I would be transferred to the Bombay office. However, Manju and our daughter had to return to Bombay on their own to meet the society's deadline. My daughter, Reshmi, was two weeks away from her first birthday. Now, mother and daughter had to celebrate Reshmi's first birthday by themselves, without me! They stayed in my lawyer friend's house for two weeks, while he had the tenant thrown out with the help of the police. The flat was cleaned up and Manju moved in with Reshmi. The very first night, the doorbell rang; it was a client of the previous brothel owner. I have mentioned earlier that my wife was a strong and confident person. Apparently, she chased him out the house; in his fright, the man left his slippers behind and ran off onto the road.

In my last week at the Calcutta office, the manager hosted a grand cocktail party to welcome the chairman of Benson Company who was visiting the offices in India. This was his first trip to India. He seemed impressed with the grand reception and the high profile of clients who came to the party. The staff that was selected to attend on the guests had to wear typical British black jackets and bow ties. I did not possess either and was asked to hire them.

My stay in Calcutta ended in early 1970. A period of two and half years was well spent. I had learnt a lot and got to understand the basic principles and intricacies of the business. I learnt that the advertising profession instils patience and tenacity in people. These qualities are put to test almost on a daily basis. They help develop an uncanny ability to understand people's behaviour and find ways of dealing with them. They face different kinds of clients and organizations and have to adapt to them without betraying any stress.

I had handled three clients for over two years: Dunlop-pillow, GEC and ABTM. Each one was a different experience. Each one covered a different set of potential buyers. Dunlop-pillow was a household product, purchased almost as a commodity. GEC radios were, on one hand, a news vehicle and on the other hand, entertainment. The third product was a lathe machine; I had no idea what it did until I visited the factory to be briefed about the product's functions.

As people, the clients differed in their behaviour. It was great fun when I had to meet all the three clients on the same day. The Dunlop-pillow gentleman was pompous person and was involved with music festivals in the city. He was quite well-known by music lovers who needed tickets for festivals at short notice. That gave him a feeling of self-importance. This attitude he carried to work as well. Mercifully, he took a liking to me. I listened to him for as long he wished to speak about the people he knew in the city. Which was why I fixed meetings with him towards the end of the day. The GEC client was fun-loving. He spoke very little about work and more about actors. GEC had the best recording equipment, which he lent to the film industry. The lathe man was very business-like. He was not a Bengali like the other two clients. For him, time was money. He always had two people waiting for him. I always preferred to visit him first thing in the morning.

I was hoping that the experiences at the Calcutta office would help me build my career further. Bombay, I was told, was a far more competitive city than Calcutta. The clients were far more demanding and at times unreasonable. They kept the agencies on their toes. I was gearing myself up to meet the challenge! At every step, I felt The Mother was guiding and enriching me with a variety of experiences that had paved the way for me to move forward.

I thanked The Mother for getting me back to Bombay.

Chapter Seven

The Up and Downs The Bombay Experience

I was asked to report at 9:00 AM to one Mr. Machado, who was a senior client-servicing executive. I informed the receptionist about the purpose of my visit. She called Mr. Machado on the intercom and told him my name. She told me, "You have to wait, he is in a meeting."

I waited for over three hours. His secretary informed me, "He has asked you to come back after lunch." I stepped out of the office to find myself something to eat by the roadside. I returned to the office at 1:45 PM. This time, I waited for an hour. Ultimately, I met him.

He spoke rapidly and explained which clients I would be handling along with him. He took less than 15 minutes. There was a definite difference in the pace of the two cities. In Calcutta, my boss took over two hours to brief me about clients. In Bombay, it had taken around 15 minutes. He asked me to report to work at 9:00 AM.

The next morning I had to take a train into the heart of town. This was my very first ride on the famous Bombay locals. I had to push my way into the compartment. Soon I realized that my purse had been stolen. I had to get off at the next station and walk home to get some money to buy the return ticket. As a result, I was half an hour late to office. I become extremely tense. You cannot join a new place and be late - it is just not done or expected! All I could do at the moment was to pray to The Mother. I reached the reception and the lady told me to wait since my boss had not come yet!

Being a large office, the structure was totally different from the Calcutta office. The two businesses I was to work on were under two different directors of the agency. I was put on the Taj hotel business and Modella - a suiting company. Hence, I would be working with two of the senior most people in the agency.

Within the next few weeks, I realized that my immediate boss was rather lazy. However, he wrote presentations very well. There was a lot to learn from him. Gradually, he let me handle clients alone. I had established good working relationships with both the clients. He would avoid visiting clients. This meant that the two directors of the agency would have to attend meetings when a client company's managing directors were present. I would go along with them. It was indeed a huge opportunity for me to learn how deal with senior clients.

Finally, I had settled down to the style of working in the Bombay office. Unlike Calcutta, where the relationship between staff was friendly and informal, the Bombay office was very business-like.

I was enjoying my work. I worked hard, and was in the office on almost all Sundays. I was lucky to have good people as my clients. I did not realize that a year had passed till a secretary from the HR department congratulated me for the completion of a year in service at the Bombay office. And to my surprise, she also handed over an increment letter.

A sudden development took place. Mr. Hawthorne, the managing director, was returning to London and was being replaced by the Calcutta manager, the first Indian to head the agency. As soon the announcement was made, the entire office was in a state of shock. The Calcutta manager had not worked in the Bombay environment which was the Mecca of advertising; and he was also junior to the other two directors who were well-respected in the industry.

A week later, the Calcutta manager moved to Bombay and took charge.

It was obvious to me that the luxurious cocktail party hosted by the manager in Calcutta the previous year for the visiting worldwide chairman of Bensons had influenced the decision. I did not tell anybody that a spectacular cocktail party was perhaps the secret behind this unexpected appointment!

I must confess that I did benefit from this change. Within a few weeks of his arrival, I was promoted to the next level. However, since the entire agency was against this appointment, it disrupted work and vitiated the atmosphere completely. The two superseded directors were at war. They began to influence the staff against the new man. They also began to persuade clients to write to the London office about how the unrest in the agency was affecting the flow of work. At another level, charges were being made about financial irregularities. Then we heard that Mr. Hawthorne was in town to sort out the mess. However, he did not visit the office and worked from his hotel room.

A few days later, a fresh announcement was made, appointing the senior-most director to head the agency. The incumbent, the Calcutta manager, was reported to have resigned. Mr. Hawthorne flew back to London. The following day, the new managing director announced the resignation of the other director. Apparently, he had decided to open his own agency.

The next morning I was called by the marketing director of Modella suiting company to meet him immediately. He seemed upset. He said, "You have not shown any courtesy to us. Are you joining this new agency?" I almost screamed in surprise, "NO!" Then he informed me that the director had told them that I was joining him. He had apparently said, "There will be continuity in the team and you will have no problem." Disturbed, I returned to the office. The peon informed me that the director wanted to see me right away. He almost blew me away with his scornful screaming. He shouted, "Who do you think you are? I will destroy your career in advertising!" My brain was just not confused but in a chaotic mess! This sudden development was beyond my comprehension. When big people get into a fight, why should small people like me get pulled into the ring!

I did not realize that there was more to follow. It was going to turn out to be even worse!

Much before I was transferred to Bombay, two other gentlemen had moved there from the Calcutta office. The three of us were invited to dinner by the outgoing managing director and his wife. We were told at dinner that he too was planning to open an agency and wanted us to join him. I am not sure whether it is permissible to say a few words about his wife. But it might help to understand why her husband had to face such humiliation. She was an ambitious and proud woman. At least once a week, she would visit the office and order the staff to do her personal errands. In sheer fear of her presence, I managed to keep away from her sight.

She brought up the topic of their new agency. The husband sat quietly.

"How can you not support the man who helped all of you to build your careers?" she asked with a great deal of passion. In a way she was right. We were trapped. The following day, the three of us submitted our resignations. That was indeed a big mistake on my part.

We all tried our best to get clients. The man from Calcutta was unknown to the industry. We struggled for six months without any breakthrough. I was running out of money. Manju and I suffered many sleepless nights. We did not share our plight with any family members. It would have troubled them and humiliated us.

We prayed to The Mother to get us out this mess. It was an emergency call for her intervention. Two days later, a registered letter arrived from my father. His younger brother had sold our old house in Hyderabad and my father had sent my share. For a few minutes we kept the cheque at The Mother's photo and expressed our gratitude for this unexpected windfall. The house had been on sale for a long time. The Mother's grace had solved two serious problems in one go! The next morning, a person from a leading newspaper called and informed me that there was a vacancy for a client-servicing executive at Thompson, the largest agency in the country. I rushed out of the flat and called the gentleman from the public booth. He asked me to come to the office at 2:00 PM.

I arrived at the reception of the largest advertising agency in the country.

The receptionist was prompt in informing the secretary of the person I was there to see. Within a few minutes a lady came and led me to the client-servicing director's room. He was young, polished, and smart and had an American accent. He offered me some coffee. He asked me about the clients I had worked with in Calcutta as well in Bombay. He asked me to call him after a week. He mentioned 'next week' which sounded quick enough to him; for me it was a long wait! People who have jobs do not understand the agonizing waiting period for the unemployed!

I was asked to come at 9:00 AM. I was to meet the manager of Bombay office. He was quite the opposite of the man I had met the previous week. From the very start, he began to discourage me from joining Thompson. He said, "It is a very big agency and has lots of people. You will get lost and will learn nothing. Think hard before you decide!" I had never faced a man like him before. I came out the room quite shaken. However, he led me to the client-servicing director's office – the gentleman I had met the previous week.

He did not ask me how the meeting with the manager went. I did not volunteer to tell him either. I was just praying to The Mother to help me, having brought me to the doorstep of a great agency.

In his usual manner, he ordered for coffee. He was clearing his throat and that made me very nervous. Was he going to shake my hand and let me go? After clearing his throat, he asked, "When can you join?"

Please forgive me but I am unable to describe my emotions at that moment except to thank The Mother with tears in my eyes. All I said was, "Now!" He was surprised because most people needed to give a month's notice to their previous employer. He said I would be working with him on the Horlicks business. This was one of the Bombay office's biggest clients. He asked me to drop by the next day to collect my appointment letter. He even saw me off at the lift.

My big lesson out the biggest mistake I made in my life was simply this: before taking any major decision, just sit down and pray to The Mother. Describe your problem to her accurately, as if she is in front of you. You will be taken by surprise when a thought suddenly enters your mind and shows you the way. Your immediate reaction is likely to be, "I never thought of that!" Of course, it was not your idea at all and that is how Her Grace works.

The next day I entered the Thompson office and stayed with the agency for 30 years. The Mother had provided me with a life-time job. Her grace turned out to be much more than just a job. It was an outstanding opportunity to learn something new every day of my life. The Mother wrote to someone in a letter, "One has always something to learn and a progress to make, and in circumstance we can find the occasion of learning the lesson and making the progress."

At that time, Thompson was perceived as the university of advertising and Horlicks, the guru of marketing. Could I dream or aspire for such a unique combination?

I began work on Horlicks the following day. It was a hectic beginning! The marketing director from London, the headquarters of the company, was visiting the agency to brief us on a new project. The document, which outlined the objective of this project, was very comprehensive and provided all the necessary details required by the agency to begin work. I had never read a more sparkling brief before.

Incidentally, the London office was very involved with the agency at all stages of work. The company had a comprehensive structure that covered all aspects of their business: the marketing director, the sales director, the research director, the distributor director and the production director. The agency was involved with each of these men. For instance, the research head from London would himself visit towns and villages to supervise the research that was being conducted by the local research agency. Horlicks treated its agency as if it was part of their company. The agency personnel working on the account were invited to their annual sales conference held at exotic places in India. Literally, from Kashmir to Kanya Kumari, different locations were selected as venues. That is how I visited many interesting places in the country.

Every meeting was a new learning for me. I took extensive notes at these meetings. I was very happy at work and was enjoying every minute I spent in the office.

Meanwhile Manju, finding me well-settled in my job, decided to study further. She studied B.Ed and completed the course in one year. She fared extremely well in her exams and was among the top 10 in her college. She began to teach in a well-known school at Juhu, in the suburbs of Bombay. She learned to drive and drove back and forth to the school every day.

One day, Horlicks announced that it was shifting its head office to New Delhi. The next day, the agency announced that my boss was being promoted as the Delhi office manager. He had been associated with Horlicks for over and a decade and half. Hence, it was not surprising that Horlicks had initiated this move.

I was lost and deeply depressed. I was too deeply involved with the Horlicks brand and hence, I just went blank. It took the agency a full one week to find a slot for me. They moved me to a new group that was formed to handle large Indian companies. The man in charge had been hired a few weeks earlier. He was the marketing manager of a large Indian company. Apparently, it was the first speculative move made by both sides: the person as well as the agency! I was introduced to my future boss. The first thing he said to me was this: "Since you have over eight years experience, I will leave it to you to manage the clients. However, make sure you do not make any mistakes. You will have to take full responsibility for them."

This was going to be totally a new experience for me: to work with a man who enjoyed all the perks and authority but no responsibility! He just drank coffee, almost by the hour, and would chat with people who had nothing to do with his clients. I was not enjoying my work and what was worse, I stopped learning as well.

Every single night, I would pray to The Mother for her intervention.

The prayer helped me to the extent that I would go to work every morning with a little more energy.

Three months later, I was called by the managing director, Mr. John Gaynor. This was my very first meeting with him. When bosses suddenly descend on you, your mind goes berserk. Was he going to sack me? Perhaps my boss might have complained about my attitude?

I got to his office. It was the size of half a tennis court.

He began, "I have got good reports about your work on Horlicks." I was wondering whether he was planning to send me to Delhi as well. Then he said that my boss had recommended me for a position that had just fallen vacant in this office. I was made a senior client-servicing person in charge of the Philips business.

He quickly moved on to another subject. He said I had been booked to fly to Delhi next morning to supervise work on the Philips's pavilion at the international fair. Dazed with this sudden development, I arrived in Delhi by the morning flight I was surprised and indeed delighted to see the Delhi office manager, my previous boss, waiting to receive me. I hugged him in gratitude. We drove straight to the exhibition site. We arrived at the Philips pavilion. The Philips's marketing director saw us arrive and came towards us and began to abuse us. "What kind of an agency do you run?" He looked at the Delhi manager and said, "Who is this man you have brought now?" To which the Delhi manager responded, "He is very good, and a hard-working person. He will take care of all the problems."

"He'd better if the agency wishes to retain our business." Then he walked away in disgust. I was shocked. I had no idea I had been pushed into a hopeless situation. Mr. Gaynor had not mentioned this. Driving back to the hotel, the manager of Delhi office explained that the person I had replaced had been fired. Philips was very angry with him due to his negligence at the Philip's pavilion. Apparently this project was critical for Philips to get the government's sanction to manufacture some of their newer products in India.

The Philips management had informed Mr. Gaynor about the complete chaos that prevailed in the pavilion. He was given an ultimatum to set things right within a week. The pavilion was to be visited by the worldwide chairman of Philips from Holland within the next ten days. Knowing nothing about Philips or its international products, I was supposed to turn things around with lightning speed!

I found a lot of people from Thompson's Bombay office chatting away at the coffee shop of a five-star hotel in Delhi. I walked towards them and enquired as to what they were doing in Delhi. A team of 35 people had been sent a week earlier to supervise work at the pavilion. None of them were at the pavilion when we went there around 6 PM to 9 PM.

I checked into my room. I sat quietly in meditation, praying to The Mother for guidance. This was an emergency! In sheer fright, I found myself speaking loudly to The Mother, detailing my plight to her. After that, I was calmer. An action plan emerged in my mind. I called the Delhi manager and requested him to shift me and the entire team to a cheaper hotel, closer to Pragati Maidan - the exhibition ground. I walked down to the coffee shop and spoke to the staff. I said, “We will all shift to another cheaper hotel tomorrow morning. Right now, I would like you all to come with me to the Philips pavilion.” They were all upset and said, “We do not report to you!” In a very quiet voice, I informed them that I had taken over from their boss.

They were shocked and took a while to absorb this information. We then left for the pavilion. Believe me, I knew nothing about exhibitions. The Philips pavilion occupied an area the size of a football field. The place was covered with huge crates of Philips’ international products. These had to be placed according to the blueprint sent by Philips, Holland. These had arrived ten days ago. I studied the plan and divided the team to work at different locations to supervise the masons, electricians and packers. This work force of over 100 people had also come from Bombay. They were lodged in a rented house, close to the pavilion.

I had asked all of them to assemble at the Philips pavilion at 8:00 AM. I waited for them for over two hours. It was 10:00 AM when they came, obviously after a sumptuous breakfast! I was at the pavilion with the supervisory staff and the workers until 3:00 AM. When we returned to the hotel, I told them we would leave at 9:00 AM for the pavilion. Mercifully, there were no protests. The Mother had given me the energy to work that day for over 16 hours!

The following morning when the Philips personnel arrived at the pavilion, they were taken by complete surprise over the progress made that night. One of them asked me, "How did you manage this turnaround?" Spontaneously, I replied," It was not me but my guru who guided me through last night." He was taken aback and asked me who he was. I instinctively said, "The Mother, of Sri Aurobindo Ashram." He turned out to be a devotee of The Mother himself who visited the Ashram quite frequently with his family! He was emotionally moved.

The pavilion was ready on time. The chairman of Philips praised the display and the workmanship. The Indian directors made a call to Mr. John Gaynor and thanked him for taking such prompt action.

I returned to the office. Mr. Gaynor came to my room and handed over a letter of promotion, an increase in salary and a company car. Believe me, I just ran into the toilet with tears flowing down my face because I did not know how to thank The Mother! But The Mother had told us many times that if you make a sincere effort, the Divine will always help you.

I worked on the Philips business as well as on many others that were added to my portfolio. More people were added to my group to meet the needs of clients. I was enjoying my work. I had an excellent team and we worked very well together. I had developed an excellent relationship with Philips at almost all levels: the directors of the company, the marketing team and even the production people.

The chief executive of Thompson Mr. Ghosal was a legend in the advertising industry, not only in India but around the world. He had received national and international awards. Mr. Ghosal was to retire within a year and had chosen the Delhi manager (my previous boss in Bombay) as his successor.

Apparently, Mr. Ghosal had decided to send me to Delhi as manager to carry forward the cordial relationship that Thompsons had enjoyed over the long years with Horlicks. However, I was told later that he had visited the marketing director of Philips to seek his agreement for my shift from their business.

Mr. Ghosal returned from the Philips office and called for me. He recounted his meeting with the marketing director. The marketing director apparently said, "If the move is good for Ram's career, we will never stand in his way."

My younger daughter, Sonali, was born in Bombay on June 30, 1975. For the second time, we had to move to another city when our daughter was one-year-old! Unfortunately, Manju had to give up her teaching career. It was a pity, because at that point in time she was offered a scholarship to do her M. Ed!

Chapter Eight

Ups and Downs
The Delhi Experience

We moved to Delhi in June 1976. We occupied a company house which had four bedrooms, two small lawns - one in the front and the other at the back. All our life we had lived in two-bedroom apartments. This was a luxury we had never dreamed or aspired for! It took a while for us to get adjusted to this life of luxury. However, two months later, the electricity bill took half my salary! I had to borrow money from the company every month. Mercifully, within three months, the company decided to increase my salary. Perhaps, it was affecting the company's cash flow!

Our move to Delhi happened one year after Mrs. Gandhi had declared a state of emergency in the country. It seemed to me as if the company timed my transfers to cities where trouble was brewing! It began with the Naxal movement in Calcutta and now in Delhi it was the drama of the Emergency unfolding! All the politicians who were against her were arrested. Newspapers faced severe censorship hence rumours and gossip took over. Within a few days of our arrival, we were invited to dinner by our neighbour. Immediately after the first round of drinks, heated discussions began against the Emergency. A gentleman was vociferous in his remarks against Mrs. Gandhi. I moved away to join the women who were talking about their children - a safe subject for discussions!

A little later, a lady was running around looking for her husband. He was nowhere to be found. The host searched all the toilets and bedrooms. Then he stepped out to ask the watchman whether anybody had left the house. The watchman said the gentleman had driven off with someone who'd come in a jeep. The party ended in chaos and anxiety. The following morning we learnt that the police, dressed as civilians, had arrested him and kept him in the prison for the night. Apparently, there was someone at the party who had informed the police about the discussions taking place against Mrs. Gandhi. After this shocking experience, we did not attend any parties, except those given by our clients or our company.

However, I faced a similar situation a few months later. An international trade exhibition was being inaugurated by the President of India. Our agency had designed a few stalls for our international clients hence I was invited to attend the inauguration along with a few clients.

We were seated in the second row, right in front of the podium. The President was reading out his speech when one of the pages of his speech flew away. He did not notice it and continued to read. As a result, his speech was totally disconnected and none of us understood it.

One of the clients turned to me and said, "Would you hire this man as an executive in your agency?" Two people tapped our shoulders and asked us to follow them. They took us to the main gate and asked us to go home. These were security men in civilian garb keeping their eyes and ears open!

Indirectly, the Emergency was affecting the advertising industry. Clients had to be extra cautious with their advertising expenditure, the content of advertisements and shop promotions. Nothing could obliquely refer to the situation relating to the Emergency.

On October 31, 1984, I was in a meeting with the managing director of Escorts Company at Faridabad. He received a call that Mrs. Indira Gandhi had been assassinated by her two Sikh guards while walking towards her office. The meeting was called off. I left for home. I was stopped at the border of Haryana and Delhi. No cars were permitted to proceed into Delhi city. I got out the car and told the driver to return home when the borders opened. I crossed the border after a personal check was done. The distance to Delhi from the border was over 20 kilometres. I had hardly walked 500 meters when a truck driver stopped and offered me a lift. The Grace was at work!

We had moved from Panch Shila Park to Greater Kailash (Part Two) just a few weeks ago. The owners of the houses on our street were predominantly Sikhs. A huge crowd had gathered on the street. They were stoning houses and breaking glass windows. Fierce riots were raging. The motive behind these riots was the assassination of Mrs. Gandhi by her Sikhs guards..

Fortunately, our house was not attacked since it did not have a nameplate at the gate. Sometimes incompetence can also benefit you. The office had forgotten to fix my name plate!

Delhi was plunged into one of its worst episodes of sectarian violence since the partition of India in 1947. I noticed that all the owners had covered their nameplates in order to conceal their identities. I got a call from one of the girls who worked in our office. There was fierce fighting on their street. They were Sikhs. I asked her to move immediately to our office guesthouse which was located in a more cosmopolitan locality. Apparently their house was partly burnt down during the night.

In a way I too was a victim of these riots. In 1981, DDA (Delhi Development Authority) was planning to build three-bedroom homes in Vasant Kunj. It was an open offer. I applied for one of these houses. I paid a sum of Rs.10,000 as an initial deposit. While the homes were being constructed, they were being allotted by a lottery. I got my house towards the end of 1983. During these riots, someone broke into the house and occupied it. My administrative manager was looking after it. When things settled down in Delhi, he paid a routine visit to the house and found it occupied. He panicked and called me. I asked him to visit the occupants and find out who they were. He called back to say, "It is a Sikh family who moved out of their rented house from an area where riots were on for safety of the family."

Manju cautioned me to handle the situation tactfully. She prayed to The Mother and allowed me go to pay a visit to the house. I took my administrative manager with me. We rang the doorbell. An elderly Sikh gentleman opened the door. I informed him that I was the owner of the house. He respectfully invited me inside. He called his wife and the rest of the family members to welcome me. It was a large family. His wife offered me some buttermilk. I hate the drink but I had to accept it to avoid any further trouble. The family withdrew from the drawing room.

The man came straight to the point. "Will you sell me your house?"

I did not think for even a moment, I blurted out," Yes!" I was surprised with my instantaneous response. He said, "You mention the price and I will pay it right away." My manager wisely intervened and said, "Sir, I will discuss with the brokers of the locality and get back to you tomorrow." The next day I quoted the price. He asked, "Do you want cash or a check?" I said, "I will take a check. I do not deal with black money." He responded, "You are a lucky man. A businessman in this country cannot deal in white money!" He gave me the check. My manager promised to deal with all the transaction papers. After this extraordinary experience, I began to respect the Sikh community. If I had to file a case to recover this property, I would have probably spent a lifetime fighting it! Apparently, my wife, according to my daughters, was meditating till the doorbell rang. That explained my immediate response to the Sikh gentleman!

At first, it was tough to get adjusted to Delhi after Bombay. There was a great difference between the two cities. For instance, in Bombay I travelled to work by the local train. I would take the 08:01 train to Church Gate station. For the return journey, the train left at 07:27 in the evening. The precision was a characteristic of Bombay. I was surprised to see the same people travelling daily at these timings. I saw the same people for over five years both ways. The value of time was written on the faces of every Bombay resident. Time translated into money.

My first week in the Delhi office was trying. The office hours were from 9:00 AM to 6:00 PM with a lunch break between 1:00 and 2:00 PM. In the Bombay office, the staff would all be in by 9:00 AM sharp.

In the Delhi office, however, I was the only one in at 8:45 AM. Most people came in at 9:30 AM. The reason was that public buses never kept to time. I was too new to convince them to start from home a little earlier. I had to establish my credibility; they owed me nothing till I proved myself!

I held a meeting with the senior people to learn more about the clients and their businesses. I began to sense that some senior person in the office was advising the others not to cooperate with me. I did not get the feedback I required to begin to run the office – either about the clients or the staff. At this point in time, my Air India experience with travellers, led me to find a way out this situation.

I had discovered that different types of people need to be treated differently. Some need to be shown courtesy and respect and others seek friendliness and approachability. I also figured that both these steps needed to be taken at the same time. These were my first two steps: I created an executive committee consisting of senior people in the office. Meetings were held every Friday morning for an hour. I wanted them to be a part of the decision-making process. The second step was simpler: I had the door-closure instrument removed and kept my room door wide open. Unlike my predecessor, nobody needed an appointment from my secretary to see me. If clients came to see me, I would move to the conference room.

My professor at the advertising course in London used to say this quite often: "Advertising is a people's business: the clients, their customers and the agency staff. You need to set up top priority to observe people's behaviour, understand and interpret them before taking any action."

From the second meeting of the executive committee I began to get a firmer understanding of our clients' businesses. The people were opening up in response to the importance they had been shown. From the second week itself, the general staff entered my room to assure me of their cooperation. Incidentally, I followed this practice for the rest my career until retirement.

The client mix in the Delhi office was challenging. I had no exposure or experience of working with government-owned companies, politicians, bureaucrats and large family-owned businesses. It was tough to deal with such a variety of people, with totally different mindsets. I had a lot to learn quickly before I got into trouble! To begin with, I had to wear clothes that fitted with the environment of the company. For instance, in both Calcutta and Bombay, I always wore suits for meetings with clients. That was the way to show respect. In Delhi, I needed to wear suits while meeting two clients: Horlicks and Nestle. I would wear a full-sleeved shirt and a tie for meetings with bureaucrats. With politicians, I wore a white khadi shirt and an inexpensive pair of trousers. They liked simplicity since at that time, it was the rule of the Janata Party!

The Janata party took two swift actions: IBM and Coke were sent away from the country. This shook the two other multinational companies in Delhi - Nestle and Horlicks. Both were our agency's most important businesses. I was worried. I seemed to be facing tough situations routinely! However, I have also realized that after every tough hurdle, I have gained invaluable experience and I have recognized The Mother's Grace at work. Nestle and Horlicks were left alone. A few senior staff at IBM were absorbed by an Indian-owned company. We got their business.

However, the worst was yet to happen. The government decided to tax advertising. This created great upheaval in the clients' businesses. They cut expenditure and it deeply affected the advertising agencies' income. I was asked by the chairman of the Advertising Association of India to fix an appointment with the finance minister. The meeting was fixed for 5:30 PM. While the chairman was making a PowerPoint presentation, we heard a loud snoring sound! The minister had obviously had a tough day. We left the document for him to read and thanked him for his time. The next day, we went to see the industry minister to sort out the tax issue. Someone had fixed the appointment for me. A delegation of senior agency heads arrived for the meeting from Bombay. I took them to the minister's house. His servant called us to follow him into the bathroom. The minister was shaving and dismissed our plea. "You people are millionaires, why do you want to make more money? Let us distribute some of it to the poor!" The meeting lasted for about four minutes! This was not the last that I would hear about the industry minister.

The minister was under great pressure from the young people of Delhi, at the exit of Coke, who said, "Life is not worth living without Coke!" In record time, the government created a cola drink and we got their advertising business. This was my first exposure to government personnel. The minister's first question was, "How soon can you launch the product in the market?" I honestly thought he had mistaken me for a distributor of soft drinks. I realized that the gentleman was totally ignorant about the processes involved in launching a product. I attempted to explain the process to him: the first step was for us to test the product among a young group of people; it might need some modification. Response, "We have finalized the product; do not get into it!" "However," I said, "We need to find a brand name, design the bottle and decide how and where you are going to distribute it." He gave me a blank look. He asked one of his assistants to bring the bottle. The shape was almost like the Coke bottle.

He gave me a piece of paper on which was scribbled, '77'! I thought he wanted us to create 77 names for them to decide. He said, "That is the brand name - 77! The minister wanted the name 77 so that people remembered that it was launched in 1977 under the Janata Party rule!" Nothing he said made any sense. I did not know how deal with it.

Then I decided that I should not buckle down and said, "Sir, when you put a number on the bottle so prominently, it will be read by the buyer as being the price of the bottle. They will know it cannot be Rs.77 but they would think it is 77 paise!" I had got him where I wanted! When he agreed with me, so did his entire team. I wished my team would agree with me in the same manner; it would save me arguments! However, he did a volte face and made me stay with 77. I told him that we could spell out 'Double Seven' as the brand name on the bottle. Double Seven was launched and collapsed within three months in the Delhi market. It could not travel beyond Delhi city. It tasted like cough syrup.

I had to now deal with the Delhi office's third largest client. It was Hamdard - the manufacturer of a range of products made as per the Unani system of medicine. It was owned by an old gentleman known in the city as Hakim Saheb. His office was located in a very old building. He sat on the third floor and climbed over 40 steps every day. To reach his building meant using all means of transport. I would travel around three kilometres by car. Then I had to take a rickshaw ride for about 15 minutes and then walk around 200 metres to get to the building. It was the most crowded street in Delhi!

It took me a lot of effort to build a relationship with Hakim Saheb. The executive who was handling his business of over 15 years had poisoned him against me. I also discovered that he was planning to create trouble for me through the union. The executive was ten years older than me and was expecting to be promoted as the general manager of the office. I met Hakim Saheb every Wednesday morning. Finally, I managed to build a relationship. This made the senior executive even more aggressive towards me and some union staff began a stir against me. He was banking on the Hamdard business to give him support. He knew I could not sack any union staff, especially under Janata Party rule. I decided not to bother about his mischief and focus on increasing the business.

I began to recruit people from Bombay. I got them from every discipline required to grow the business: creative persons, strategic planners and several client-managing executives. It was the best team among the Delhi agencies. This team won a lot new businesses: Oberoi hotels, Indian Airlines and DCM. They also created an advertising campaign to encourage young people to join the Indian Army. A lot of new clients from other agencies came to our agency. Our profitability was growing every year.

Before I joined the Delhi office, my predecessor had taken on the advertising business for TVs made by the Haryana government. It failed. They ran up a huge bill and did not have the money to settle the agency's outstanding. The board of directors had asked me to solve this problem. It must be fun being a director of the company - they do not have anything to do but boss around! Fortunately, a senior executive who worked in our agency knew Rajiv Gandhi and his family very well. I called him to my room, shared the problem and requested him to set up a meeting for me with Rajiv Gandhi. I told him that if the work got done, I would get his car painted, which was in bad shape! I met Rajiv Gandhi at his office the next day. He asked me to address a letter to Mrs. Indira Gandhi. I sent the letter to his office in the afternoon. The next day, his secretary called and asked me to meet with the Chief Minister of Haryana in the afternoon at Chandigarh.

I drove down and reached the Chief Minister's office at 4:00 PM.

As soon I reached his office, I was ushered into the Chief Minister's cabin. I saw another gentleman seated there too. I narrated my story. The Chief Minister listened and looked at the man sitting there. The gentleman began explaining the serious financial situation and the number of people the company owed monies to. I guessed he must be the chairman of the failed company. The Chief Minister rang a bell and requested his secretary to give me some tea in his waiting room. Within a few minutes, I was called back. The Chief Minister asked me to accompany the chairman to his office.

As we were driving to his office, the chairman said, "You should have come to see me. The Chief Minister pulled me up since he had received the instructions from Mrs. Gandhi's office." I kept quiet as I was waiting for the end result. I got the cheque for the total payment due to the agency.

I began to enjoy Delhi. Both my daughters got admission in Modern School, the most reputed school at that point in time. I was entitled to four weeks holiday every year. We travelled extensively by car and plane across Northern India: Kashmir, Ladakh, Rajasthan, Kulu and Manali, Madhya Pradesh, Uttar Pradesh, Jim Corbett Park, Kedarnath and Badrinath.

I had a hectic work schedule in Delhi. I had very little time for the family. My wife, Manju, took on the entire responsibility of bringing up the daughters. Being a qualified teacher, she helped them through their studies. She was a sitar play herself, but enrolled both the daughters in a well-known classical dancing school when they were just six-years-old. She would pick them up from their school and take them to the dance classes thrice a week. She also taught them something very important: she taught them to pray to The Mother every morning before they left for school.

Even today, both our daughters continue to pray to The Mother before they go to their respective offices in two different cities.

A painful memory of my time in the capital was what happened at the World Management Conference, which was held in Delhi. Top management gurus were invited to address the conference. I was working with the team of people who were responsible for the conference. It was inaugurated by the Prime Minister, Mr. Morarji Desai. His opening speech was a disaster. He ran down the idea of foreigners coming to India to advise us on how to manage the country. He looked towards a large audience of foreigners and said, "Go to our villages and see how they happy they are. They do not need any help or advice from management scholars!"

He was followed by the industry minister who was even worse. He told the audience that they were all rats. He said, "Each one of you is spending thousands of rupees to stay in luxury hotels in a poor country. And that does not seem to hurt your conscience!" We all witnessed the shocking sight of Dr. Peter Drucker leave the hall. He was the keynote speaker of the conference. He had flown all the way from New York to address 1,500 people: all senior managers from major industries in India.

We had great difficulty in persuading him to address the audience after the coffee break. We assured him that both those gentlemen had left. As he entered the hall, he received a standing applause from the delegates.

We all came to the conclusion at the end of the conference, that Delhi was not the ideal city to hold international conferences. It was dominated by haughty and arrogant politicians and bureaucrats!

Right through my career, during brief intervals, I had to face some concern or the other. Corporate life, at times, would seem like a battlefield where everyone believes they are born winners! Petty politics was an everyday pastime.

Some sudden developments took place in the company. An American advertising agency in India went broke and wished to sell it. They approached the Thompson Company in New York to buy their 40% overseas share and the Indian company to take over the balance 60%.

What I gathered from media sources was that the agency, at one time, was doing well and had quite a few international and national clients. It had a network of four offices across the country. Apparently, the root cause of its decline was mismanagement. The Chief Executive had some personal problems with his family which turned him into an alcoholic.

Incidentally, this was the first deal in the advertising industry where one agency was bought over by another. Over the last two decades, it has become a fashion. Now there are companies that are raiding and buying over half a dozen agencies at a time!

I was called for a meeting in Bombay. The board of directors decided, in consultation with New York office, to appoint me as the president and CEO of this bankrupt agency! However, the name of the agency was changed to Contract Advertising Private Limited. This was indeed a consolation and a good way to change the face of the agency. I made a request for a second senior executive from the Delhi office to be the manager of Contract. They readily agreed.

All my well-wishers advised me against accepting this position. To them, it seemed like punishment for a job well done. They had a good reason to feel that way. Two other large agencies had created smaller second agencies with the hope that they would be able take on conflicting businesses in order to increase the overall profits of the group. These second agencies were struggling to stay alive.

However, the consolation was that I was being seconded from the parent company to run this new outfit and would remain on the payroll of the parent company. Of course, it goes without saying, that if I failed I would be given a more junior position in the parent company. It meant I was getting into it with somewhat negative thoughts.

As was my usual practice, I sat in meditation and prayed to The Mother. I was reminded of what The Mother said once, "You can overcome any difficulty if you work sincerely and the Divine's Grace will help you."

My attitude changed slightly and I felt a little more positive about the new assignment.

We had completed ten years in Delhi. It certainly was one of the happiest times of our lives.

I accepted the position and moved back to Bombay in 1986. I was due to retire in the next twelve years. This seemed the last lap of my working life!

Chapter Nine

Back to Bombay to Face a Challenging Task

It is a rather a strange phenomenon that whenever I have moved from one city to another, people have attempted to scare me. When I was moving from Calcutta to Bombay, people said it was a tough city to live in. They warned me that I would find it difficult to adjust to moving out of a friendly city to a fiercely competitive and demanding city. The move to Delhi from Bombay was even more frightening. It was said that nothing moves in Delhi except cars! And when I was moving back to Bombay from Delhi, people said, "Bombay is totally changed. It is not any more what it was a decade ago!"

Nothing could be scarier to me than the task handed over to me. It had become a habit with me to get started right away when faced with a serious problem. I discovered that plunging into it helped in avoiding nervousness. This is exactly what I did the very first day in Bombay. I wrote an advertisement which was released the day

I joined the agency. It was April 1. "April Fool's day! If you are as crazy as we are, join Contract Advertising for creative adventure!" We got a few applications and some coverage in the media.

As a result, I got the opportunity to make some friends in the media. I asked them why two second agencies belonging to two large agencies had not succeeded. The information was most important for me to plan my strategy. Two main reasons were: the senior managers sent out on deputation continued to use the parent companies' visiting cards, while the rest of the staff carried the second agency's cards. This obviously meant they were not distancing themselves from the parent company. Moreover carrying parent company visiting cards would not get them conflicting business. Apparently, they needed clearance from the parent agency to go pitch for a business which was in conflict with theirs. Simply stated, they did not enjoy independent status as an agency!

In the first board meeting I clarified my stand: I would use Contract Advertising visiting cards and I should be allowed to pitch for conflicting businesses. Except for one director, the rest of them agreed with my request.

My first hour was spent with the finance manager. The balance sheet figures were much worse than what I had been informed. It shocked me. I struggled to understand the situation of the agency; it was left with practically no client who was spending money on a regular basis. It had four offices: Bombay, Delhi, Calcutta and Madras.

The next meeting was with the HR head. He was reluctant to tell me the number of employees the agency had across the four offices. He had been with the agency for over 25 years and never seemed to have recommended to the management that they reduce the staff.

I grasped the problem but did not know where to begin. I was facing an impossible position and my mind was making it even worse. It was throwing in contradictory ideas and adding to my nervousness and helplessness. Invariably, when I find myself in trouble, I automatically recall The Mother's words. She had said when you are confused, sit in silence; make every effort to drive away the negative thoughts and await the Divine Grace. It was tough but finally I got some positive ideas. I scribbled a plan of action and left it on the table. I decided to sleep over it and study it the next day. Often I have become enthusiastic with ideas and keen to implement them. However, with experience, I have discovered that I needed to let the ideas take a final shape before I went forward. To hurry is not always the best solution.

The next step was to invite the office managers for a meeting in Bombay. I was genuinely sympathetic towards them. If the overall image of the agency takes a beating, it is almost impossible for the manager of any city to keep it going. It was gracious of them to move out within a few months to give the new management space to make some changes. We thereafter added six top creative people across the offices. They loved the idea of creative adventure!

I held a two-day conference at a sea resort. The senior people in the agency - senior client-servicing persons and creative directors - of all the office were invited to attend. At the end of the meet, we all agreed that our key focus would be to create outstanding ideas for our clients. I ended up by challenging all of them to make Contract the most creative agency in the industry. I suggested a five-minute meditation and requested them to pray to The Mother. I had carried a large photo of The Mother with me to the resort, which was decorated with flowers in the conference hall.

Having got a top team together, we launched an aggressive drive to find clients. Uninvited, we went into organizations and made creative presentations. The entire agency was working 24/7 for over two months and made 20 new business pitches. These high-energy-level pitches landed us in trouble. Agencies complained to the advertising agency associations against us. They felt it was highly unethical to chase other people's clients. The president of the association, who was CEO of the second largest agency, called me for a meeting. He kept me waiting for about 30 minutes at the reception area of his office. Apparently, he had commented, "This fellow from Delhi needs to be fixed." I was wondering what I should say in my defence. At that moment a senior media person walked in. He sat down and asked me about the purpose of my visit. I told him why I had been summoned. Pat came his response. "Just ask him what he would do if he was in your position." I must confess that I had never thought of that. The Divine Grace does work in strange ways! Can one pass it off as mere coincidence?

I was called in and asked, "Why are you breaking the association's rules and creating chaos in the industry?'

"Sir, you are a very respected professional and I wish to seek your advice in this matter. I have been given a task; what would you have done if you were in my position?"

He waited for a few minutes and said, "I would do exactly what you are doing!"

We shook hands and he wished me success. People never seem to place themselves in situations on which they pass judgments on others.

Meanwhile, we won half of the businesses we had pitched for!

The media was carrying news about our business gains.

The mood of the agency had changed from a sense of insecurity to a state of well-being.

On Friday, March 12, 1993, I returned from Delhi and was driving from the airport to the office. My office was situated opposite the Regional Passport Office in Worli. I got out of the car and walked up to the first floor and entered my office. Exactly ten minutes later, I heard a very loud noise. I rushed to the balcony attached to my room. It was a massive bomb explosion. A double-decker bus was on fire with passengers screaming for help. Many dead bodies were lying on the road and several injured people were crying out loud in pain.

My secretary came running, yelling out, "Sir, get in!"

I asked her, "Helen, what the hell is going on here?"

She informed me that the first bomb blast had taken place at Nariman Point, the business headquarters of

Bombay. Thereafter, apparently 13 bomb blasts took place, covering places from the south to the north sides of the city. It was sparked off by the controversy over the destruction of the Babri Masjid at Ayodhya. After recovering from the shock, I walked around the office to find that all the air conditioners had fallen on the road. Most of the glass cabins were shattered. When I returned to my cabin, I found some senior executives waiting for me. They looked at me and pointed towards The Mother's photograph displayed in my room and said, "Sir, She saved you. If you were a few minutes late, you would have been blown off!" Apparently, two cars had burnt down with passengers inside them.

Within a year of settling down at Contract, another dramatic development took place. Mr. Martin Sorrell, former finance director of the famous British agency, Saatchi & Saatchi (the two brothers) who took the advertising world by storm, resigned from his job. He bought a small company called, Wire & Paper Products - WPP, which supplied baggage trolleys to the airports in England.

In 1986, he began his expedition of acquiring advertising agencies. The first agency he bought was J. Walter Thompson (that's us!) For a start, he owned 40% of Thompson and 40% of Contract Advertising as well. However, when the government regulations of ownership changed, WPP owned 100% of the two agencies. His expedition picked up rapid momentum: he bought Ogilvy in 1989, Y&R in 2000 and Grey Advertising in 2000. Thereafter, it was difficult to keep count of his acquisitions: research agencies, media agencies, digital agencies and, now I understand, he is also buying a Chinese company. I really do not know what the company does! This altered our ways of managing the agency. The agencies were under the control of his finance managers posted across the world. He also had direct access to all the major clients around the world. He was a tough taskmaster. We all had to quickly learn how to deal with the man. He was indeed a tough nut to crack!

I believe he liked to keep you on your toes! However, he could be likeable if he liked you. How did he choose the people he should like? Quite simple really: he liked aggressive people who knew how to acquire new clients. He liked me because he came to know that I was chasing everybody else's clients.

Six years after Contract was founded, A&M Magazine (Advertising & Marketing Magazine) awarded me the 'Person of the Year' award. This was the citation on the plaque given to me.

ADVERTISING PERSON OF THE YEAR

"Nominated RAM SEHGAL for making a small agency, leading it out of the shadow of its larger parent and turning it into a national institution."

At this point in time, I need to state, with full humility at my command that I cannot take credit for this award. All my life, I have been an average person. I knew from the very start of this assignment that I could never turn around this sick agency into glowing health through my own efforts. I do not intend to underplay the gigantic effort that every single member in the agency put in. I know in my heart that it was The Mother's direct intervention and her Grace that helped us achieve this herculean task. I took the plaque and placed it at the Samadhi as gratitude and homage to The Mother.

The following year, Contract Advertising was declared the Agency of the Year for its outstanding creative work. What's more, in just seven years, it was one of the top five agencies in India.

I was to retire in 1998 when I would be 60-years-old. Sir Martin extended my stay at Contract by two years. We had planned to shift to Pondicherry... Manju was disappointed; she had been keen to get back home.

Meanwhile, her older sister, Ira rang up Manju from Pondicherry and informed her about a plot of land that was on sale in a prime location. I did not have enough money to buy the land. Both the sisters were rather disappointed. A month later her sister called again. My response was the same - no money! A few weeks later, I got a call from my bank that some money had been transferred to me from London. They requested me to come across to the bank. The payment had come from WPP headquarters. They had paid me a special bonus! That money made it possible for me to buy the plot and build a house in a prime location! The Mother had told us both, "This is your home, come back!" We obeyed her and she had provided us a home!

Finally, in 2000, I was released from my responsibility of running Contract. The same year, the Advertising Club of Calcutta inducted me into its Hall of Fame.

The citation read as follows:

"To smoothly making the transition from the Ashram to advertising, for successfully bringing the agency out of the shadow of its parent, for nurturing and growing the agency and its people, for fusing creative skills with strategic strengths and making an independent entity out a subsidiary."

ADVERTISING CLUB OF CALCUTTA

IS PRIVILEGED TO INDUCT INTO ITS

HALL OF FAME

RAM SEHGAL

A PEOPLE'S PROFESIONAL

We were getting ready to leave for Pondicherry and began packing. Out of the blue I got a call. I was being offered an assignment by an agency which was owned by an Indian, in which WPP has minority shares. Sir Martin persuaded me to take the offer. I accepted the offer for two reasons: the house would take two years to build and honestly speaking, the offer was too tempting to be turned down! It also gave me an opportunity to work with Japanese companies for the first time and also deal with Japan's largest agency - Dentsu. I had worked with American, British, French, German and Swiss companies. I would have missed out this opportunity of learning. It took me to Japan twice a year to attend management meetings as guests of the Japanese agency. There was a lot to learn from Japan: the grace and hospitality of their people; the civilized way they conduct their business; the respect they show to even junior employees. It was amazing to see how well-prepared they were for meetings. Japanese companies never sack any employee - it is a lifetime employment. Hence, there is always continuity with the person you are dealing with. I thoroughly enjoyed my work with this agency.

I stayed there for five years. I had overstayed by seven years; I should have been home when I hit sixty and not sixty-seven.

I finally packed up and dispatched my household goods to Pondicherry, including the car the company had given me as a gift!

Chapter Ten

The Travel Experiences

To date, my wife and I have travelled to 62 countries in the last 50 years. That did not prevent us from being nervous at the start of every journey. And all our journeys begin with a prayer to The Mother. In our prayers, we do something very important: we let The Mother know the exact plan of our journey.

There was an instance when I was working with Air India - our flight was taking off from Teheran on our way to London when one of the engines caught fire. The captain of the flight was one of the most experienced pilots in Air India. He managed to abort the take-off and saved the lives of 170 passengers. I was able to hold on to my faith and pray to The Mother to save us.

Once while landing at London airport, the undercarriage did not descend. The airport declared an emergency and asked the pilot to stay in the air while they set up the runway for an emergency landing. It was a nightmare that lasted for 90 minutes. Every passenger on the flight was screaming in fear. There were only two passengers in first class - a lady and myself. The lady was howling in fear. I went and sat next to her. I noticed that she was wearing a ring with The Mother's symbol. I showed her my ring, which was exactly like hers. I told her, "Let us pray to The Mother." She became quiet and closed her eyes.

Our flight landed safely and over 190 passengers were saved.

There have been many occasions when we have encountered minor emergencies which required The Mother's immediate intervention. On a visit to China, we went to Xian. The terracotta soldiers and their horses exhibited there dated back to 3000 B.C. Xian was also considered to be among the oldest cities in the world. It was nominated as the eighth wonder of the world.

We flew back from Xian to Beijing to catch our connecting flight to India. The transit halt was 90 minutes. We had to move from the domestic terminal to the international terminal. There were no signs in English to indicate the directions. We could not find anybody at the airport who could understand English. We roamed about helplessly trying to find our way. We were now left with 25 minutes to reach the departure gate. We silently prayed to The Mother and informed her about the details of our predicament. A few minutes later a young Chinese porter, who knew a little English, appeared and offered to help. He took us to our departure gate by a shorter route. I hugged him and gave him 50 dollars! We were the last passengers to board the flight!

Once, at Frankfurt airport, I was standing in the immigration queue when a gentleman behind me asked, "Is this line meant for departure to New York?" I turned to him and said, "Yes, it is." An immigration officer walked up to me and asked me to follow him into an empty room. He began to ask me a barrage of questions: "How do you know this man?" I said, "I don't know him at all!" He asked for my passport and boarding pass. He asked me the purpose of my visit to New York. I said I was visiting my head office for a meeting. He asked me the name of the company, the telephone number and the person I was supposed to meet.

I normally kept only my passport and the plane boarding pass in my jacket pocket. All the office papers were kept in the suitcase. Hence, his query about the office telephone number in New York made me very nervous. It was virtually impossible to remember those complicated numbers. Just to mention the company name would not have helped. I still do not remember why I was searching for it in my jacket pocket. The office telex confirming the meeting and time was in the pocket!

You cannot fool around with immigration officers in any country. They enjoy a lot of power. He went out for a minutes and returned and said, "Have a good trip!" It was obvious that he had called my office in New York to ascertain my status. I asked him, "What was it all about?" He said that the man I had been speaking to was a suspected terrorist! His parting advice was, "Never speak to a stranger at any airport in the world." I never ever deviated from his advice.

Manju also had her share of experiences with a female immigration officer at Moscow airport. I was in the men's line, while she was in the women's line. The woman officer kept turning the pages of her passport repeatedly. Granted that the passport had many world visas, but what was she suspecting? Perhaps that Manju was an agent of the drug mafia! The lady officer had sent a woman into the investigation room just before Manju came to her window. I was cleared within less than five minutes, Manju was held up much longer. I could see her lips moving and knew that she was praying to The Mother for help. Her passport was stamped, she joined me. The problem was more serious because the Russians do not speak English or French. And we knew no Russian. If any questions were asked of us and we had remained silent, that would have made them suspicious.

When one gets out of an immigration drill, the next important stop is the security check. I was wearing a lower-back support belt since I had a problem with my lower back. While the officer was making a physical check, he suddenly screamed and a few other officers came rushing. They hurriedly took me into a room and stripped me naked. They thought I had a bomb hidden in the belt! Meanwhile, in their misplaced anxiety, they damaged my protective back belt completely. I hold the same opinion about security staff as I do about immigration officers - these two groups of people are the most important and powerful people in any airport in the world!

The last part of travelling ends at the conveyor belt where prayer takes over for the safe arrival of our bags. My wife and I begin our prayer to The Mother as soon as we reach the baggage counter. We've had many mishaps – our bag not arriving on the flight; someone else taking our bag by mistake or we've taken someone else's bag by mistake.

We were travelling to Cape Town once and had a night halt at Johannesburg. We checked into a hotel close to the airport. Our flight was at 8:00 AM the next day. I opened my suitcase to take out some clothes. But Manju could not open hers. We called the hotel staff for help. They had to break open the bag. We discovered that it was not her bag. We had picked up a wrong bag since the size and colour was identical to hers. I came across a visiting card. The bag belonged to a Japanese man. We called the airline. The counter was closed. I called our travel agent in Bombay for help. She could not get through to them either. We panicked. We were beginning our travel of South Africa early the next day. How could we travel without Manju's suitcase? We were at a dead end! Some half an hour later, while we sat in prayer, Manju said, "Let us go to the airport with the bag." We took the hotel shuttle bus to the airport around 11:00 PM. We enquired about the 'Lost and Found' department. We found it and met the officer in charge. After he saw the bag and heard our story, he lost his temper.

He said, "It belonged to a Japanese man who cried when he could not find his bag. All his important business papers were in his suitcase." Meanwhile, Manju, who was standing in the corridor, noticed a trolley full of suitcases being carried away. She suddenly spotted her suitcase. She screamed and called me. I ran out and the officer came out too. He gave us the bag and asked me to write a note of apology to the Japanese gentleman.

Once when I had gone to Nairobi on work, I waited for my bag to arrive for over 30 minutes. The conveyer belt stopped, which was the signal that there were no more bags to be delivered. I registered a complaint and provided the name and phone number of the hotel.

I checked into the hotel and took the lift to go to my room. My suitcase was in the lift with a foreigner. I gently told him, "I think this is my bag." He examined it closely and shouted, "It is indeed not mine!" A worried gentleman got off the lift in a hurry!

In spite of all the panicky moments we have faced on various travels over the years, we were never scared of travelling again. The Mother's Grace has steered us through all the uncertain moments.

Faith is knowledge of the heart, beyond the reach of reason or proof. Invariably, when one faces a situation where reason cannot get you out of trouble, faith takes over.

Prayer for us, has always been an attitude of dependency on The Mother's Grace. The occurrences that surprise you are not a series of coincidences. For one who has faith, no explanation is necessary.

Chapter Eleven

The Homecoming

My return home began with some uncertainties. The same worry that plagues retired people: what should I do now?

I had lived a busy life for over 40 years. I had worked six days a week. I was away from home two weeks a month. I travelled extensively on work. Retirement meant being tired twice over: the first time, one is tired at work and the second time, one is tired of not working! It is also quite ironical that when a man retires, his company or his colleagues, gift him an expensive watch! How ridiculous can one get when all the retired person has, is time on his hands!

However, it was heartening to be welcomed by all those who grew up with us and those who knew us as children. Their affection helped us to settle down fairly quickly to the life we had lived in the early part of our stay at the Ashram.

I decided to open an advertising institute which I ran for three years. Most the students were from the Ashram and were looking for a career in advertising.

Thereafter, I was approached by a government ladies college to teach mass communication to undergraduates as an additional subject. I taught there for three years. One evening, while meditating in the Ashram, a question kept hovering in my head. When The Mother told us, "Come back, this is your home," did she mean just a physical location or was it something much deeper? I struggled for weeks, examining why I had developed this uneasy feeling. These words began to appear in my mind: all these years your life has been controlled by external factors and happenings. Now return to the spiritual life - a life of change.

I gave up all my teaching assignments.

It became obvious to me that I had returned with excess baggage, with things that had no value in the pursuit of a spiritual life. I began a critical self-analysis. I was quite astounded with my findings: a list of short-comings in the background of what Sri Aurobindo and The Mother expected of us.

I also began to analyze my journey of 40 years. At first, it looked like a zigzag – almost a random way of travel. However, pondering over it for a few months. I realized it was a journey planned by The Mother. At every step, whenever a change was required, it seemed to occur rather dramatically. If one has unshakeable faith, then in life there is no such thing as a bad experience, because everything is a valuable learning.